THE *Spirituality*
OF GARDENING

for ARI

THE *Spirituality* OF GARDENING

DONNA SINCLAIR

Northstone

Concept: Northstone Team
Editor: Michael Schwartzentruber
Industry consultant: Don Burnett, Bylands Nursery, Kelowna, BC
Cover and interior design: Margaret Kyle
Proofreading: Dianne Greenslade
Photo credits: see page 159

NORTHSTONE PUBLISHING is an imprint of WOOD LAKE
BOOKS INC. Wood Lake Books acknowledges the financial support
of the Government of Canada, through the Book Publishing Industry
Development Program (BPIDP) for its publishing activities.

WOOD LAKE BOOKS is an employee-owned company, committed
to caring for the environment and all creation. Wood Lake Books
recycles, reuses, and encourages readers to do the same. Resources
are printed on recycled paper and more environmentally friendly
groundwood papers (newsprint), whenever possible. The trees used
are replaced through donations to the Scoutrees For Canada Program.
A percentage of all profit is donated to charitable organizations.

Library and Archives Canada Cataloguing in Publication
Sinclair, Donna, 1943-
The spirituality of gardening/Donna Sinclair.
Includes bibliographical references.
ISBN 1-896836-74-7
1. Gardening – Religious aspects. 2. Gardening –
Environmental aspects. 3. Gardens – Religious aspects.
4. Spiritual life. I. Title.
BL629.5.G37S55 2005   635'.01   C2005-903489-0

Published by Northstone Publishing
an imprint of WOOD LAKE BOOKS, INC.
9025 Jim Bailey Road, Kelowna, BC, Canada, V4V 1R2
250.766.2778
www.northstone.com
www.woodlakebooks.com

Printing 10 9 8 7 6 5 4 3 2 1
Printed in Canada by Friesens

Contents

Dedication
To Jim, the compost king,
with all my heart.

Acknowledgments

Many people have been wonderfully helpful as I wrote this book. Diana Godwin, whose orphan seedlings are one marvelous gift, and her skilled advice another. Wanda and John Wallace are a source of inspiration in terms of gardening, photography, and care for the common good. I am always in awe of, and grateful for, Wanda's work with Heritage Gardeners.

Thanks to Kathy and Alan Aylett for thinking I know about gardening and for insisting I read from my current book at dinner parties, which gave me confidence to write this one. Thanks to Sarah Tector for great gardening days and so much more.

Thanks to Muriel Duncan as always, for courage. And to David Hallman for his hope that remains luminous, even though he understands what climate change could mean. Patricia Thompson's gifts of poems are a blessing.

Trisha Mills, passionate gardener, kindly watches over my seedlings in spring and gardens in summer, when I have to be away. Gardeners Jane Howe and Elizabeth Frazer cultivate my soul as well. And my brother Larry Knapp and sister-in-law Rhea Knapp share perennials and wisdom. I am always grateful for the loving care of all these people.

Thanks to George Nichol for the shared enthusiasm for plants, especially the proliferating Siberian iris. Hal Falk has kept our beloved maple alive for 15 years and we are grateful every season. Thanks to Suzanne and Bernie Brooks of Gulliver's Quality Books and Toys, for knowing that gardening books are important and for being loyal to their writers. And as always, of course, many many thanks to all the staff at Northstone Publishing. I am especially grateful to editor Mike Schwartzentruber for his patience and skill; and to designer Margaret Kyle, intuitive, creative and equally patient.

I'm grateful to my faraway children David and Joan, Andy, and Tracy for remembering to ask about the garden (in season) as a reliable clue to my health; and to my mother, Margaret Knapp, for figuring out, at the age of 91, what a writer really does all day. Thanks to Jim for putting me in charge of stuff that grows, while he does stuff that decays.

Above all, I gratefully remember my father and his garden. The love of all things green is the finest legacy, one that will last my whole life.

Introduction

I am writing this book in winter, which is when gardeners reflect. We think back with pleasure on the nicotiana's astonishing scent, the clematis winding purple and untouched through the sharp thorns of a shrub rose. It is a slow time and it reminds me that distance, looking back in peacefulness, is part of our spirituality.

But what precisely is spirituality? My dictionary says it means "of, from, or relating to God; of, concerned with or affecting the soul." I am a woman who attends church and I believe that many people connect there with a divine presence, an experience we call spiritual.

But gardens are spiritual in a different way. Although the faith I received from my ancestors is Christian, the spirituality of the garden is not attached to any one faith. That's why this book, while it refers to the Bible and to the Talmud, also turns to ancient Greece and to Native spirituality. The stories that illuminate the long relationship of the people of earth with their Creator are many and varied, and belong to all.

I've made an odd discovery. Every time I talk to a savant I feel quite sure that happiness is no longer a possibility. Yet when I talk with my gardener, I'm convinced of the opposite.

— BERTRAND RUSSELL

*A garden isn't meant
to be useful.
It's for joy.*
– RUMER GODDEN

And by gardens I mean *attainable* gardens: not the Butchart Gardens or the Edwards Gardens, or any of the great botanical wonders that we love to walk in and admire. The gardens referred to in this book are the ones that surround our homes, that greet us in the morning when we step outside the door; that peer in – as mine do – in the form of vines creeping around the windows, or boxes and containers that line steps and sit on windowsills.

I am writing about our own gardens.

I know that in mine I *connect* with God. That surely is a spiritual matter. In my garden, I understand the natural world to be part of God, something God encompasses. I suppose the natural world is not the whole of God. Theologians tell me that to equate God with nature is a heresy. This doesn't worry me

very much. In any case, I am pleased to imagine that God is larger even than our beautiful earth.

I also know that spirituality has something to do with *harmony* and *balance*. I believe in moderation; experience has taught me the value of Aristotle's golden mean. At the same time, life demands passion and single-mindedness. The twin components of calm and flame are both required. So gardeners sleepily watch the changing sun for hours from the hammock, or – heart on fire – they rise at first light to plant, or to march forth resolute at midnight intent on annihilating slugs.

Further, spirituality is founded on *history* – ancestors, ghosts, the past – as well as on the present and the future. Religion has taught me this. A spirituality that has no sense that we are the inheritors of our ancestors' generous care and the guardians of our great-great-grandchildren's future is not a spirituality at all. It is merely selfish navel-gazing. First Nations farmers, saving the seeds of a thousand varieties of maize, teaching their children the ceremonies of planting time, carefully looking after the land, have taught me this.

True spirituality is *healing*. Gardeners know this. It is why my father went to his garden during times of trouble. Working hard, feeling the muscles in your shoulders stretch, noting the death of day lily blossoms and the endless opening of new ones offers a long view. These lilies do not worry and yet they are glorious.

A day so happy.
Fog lifted early.
I worked in the garden.
Hummingbirds were
stopping over honeysuckle
flowers.
There was no thing on
earth I wanted to possess.
I know no one worth
my envying him.
– Czeslaw Milosz, *Gift*

13

Indeed, simply turning over the compost is to marvel at nature's cycle of decay and renewal. The annual transformation of dead stalks and leaves into rich soil causes my husband to lead guests to the enormous heap he has created at the very back of our yard, behind the spruce trees. All manner of miniature creatures munch happily there, creating a miracle. Visitors to our yard are not released until they have acknowledged this remarkable fact. This celebration of death and new life, this celebration of *hope*, is without doubt spiritual in nature.

No spirituality continues without *practice*. Gardening is filled with spiritual practice, the repeated rituals that draw us closer to God. There is the body prayer of bending to plant and weed, the whispered prayer at the presence of angels, the incantations of thanksgiving by those who gather and share beauty and food.

Finally, spirituality – connecting with a gentle God – is *revolutionary* in a world that worships profit. As more and more we see our world as Gaia – one single organism, the living and sacred earth – gardeners become restless. We see, for instance, governments intent on licensing for harvest every forest, the lungs of the planet. In the face of self-destructive impulse, gardeners say no.

Their efforts to save and create what is useful and lovely are deeply subversive. There is another way to live, gardeners say silently, watching the changes in the climate over the decades.

We could live our days in gratitude for all that gives us life: rain, sun, earth, and every plant from moss to trees. From the ash tree, says the Norse story of creation, Odin created the first man; and from the elm, the first woman. The universe itself is sustained by the great ash called Yggdrasil.

The earth brought forth vegetation, say the ancient authors of Genesis, describing Eden: plants yielding seed of every kind, and trees of every kind bearing fruit with the seed in it. And God saw that it was good.

That's what this book is about. The goodness and spirituality of our gardens. I believe our gardens to be more than dry soil and cedars huddled against the foundation of our homes; more even than the glorious color and texture, shape and form of a well-loved border that draws passersby to wonder. Gardens are our connection to the land and to the One who created it. They are autobiography, memory, and hope. Gardeners strive to re-create Eden on their own small pieces of earth.

In fact, the whole earth is a garden and what we learn on our little plots we bring to the larger landscape of creation. We cannot help doing this. Those who have been flung out of Eden – and that is all of us – constantly seek a return. In the words of one refugee, from among the multitude of Central American *campesinos* making the dangerous return to their villages in the 1980s, "We must go home. Our children are forgetting how to plant the corn."

There are points of time, of
distant memory,
when the soul unites
within the pattern of
the universe.
That union brings forth
the understanding of
life's harmony.
So it should be within
the garden…
— AUTHOR UNKNOWN

1
Gardening as Connection

*Now the Lord God planted a garden in the east,
in Eden…*

As a small child, I remember leaning over the side of our rowboat, letting my hand trail in the water. And I remember happiness; a powerful sense that I, and the water and the boat and the trees on the not-distant shore, were one.

As I grew older, I put away such childish things.

But I believe that the passion for gardening that I now enjoy is linked to the experience of that four-year-old mystic, to the truth she sensed. I believe gardeners yearn to reconnect with Eden. We are trying to discover a way back to that physical unity with the land still experienced by a few indigenous people, a few monks, a few mystics. One haunting story goes like this:

In the beginning, after the Lord God the Creator had made the first human from a bit of earth, God planted a garden. It was in Eden, in the east. Then, out of the ground, the Creator made to grow every tree that is pleasant to the sight and good for food, the tree of life also, in the midst of the garden, and the tree of the knowledge of good and evil.

But soon the humans ate of that tree of knowledge; and God knew they might reach out also to the tree of life, and eat, and live forever.

So the Lord God sent the humans forth from the Garden of Eden, to till the ground from which they were taken. And at the east of the Garden of Eden, God placed cherubim, and a sword flaming and turning to guard the way to the tree of life.

We were made from earth, says that story, retold from Genesis. And despite our best efforts with formaldehyde and coffins of steel, we will be earth again one day. The yearning for that ancient connection is manifest in my garden.

This we know.
The earth does not belong to us;
we belong to the earth.
This we know.
All things are connected
like the blood which unites one family.
All things are connected.
Whatever befalls the earth
befalls the children of the earth.
We did not weave the web of life,
we are merely a strand in it.
Whatever we do to the web,
we do to ourselves.

— ATTRIBUTED TO CHIEF SEATTLE

CONNECTING WITH TREES AND EARTH

It's counterproductive for a gardener to plant trees. They'll just grow up and shut off the sun. But I cannot have enough of them. Author Carolyn Heilbrun, describing her search for her own womanly space in *The Last Gift of Time*, declared she wanted a farmhouse in an open field, because trees just die and break your heart.

I confess to a strong sense of kinship with a maple that was here long before we bought our old house in a small city in Northern Ontario. And it *does* break my heart, constantly losing branches and causing me to worry about the neighbor's roof. But I also feel the maple's care for me, cooling the house and yard in the hottest summer and raining scarlet leaves in the fall.

I am grateful for it and transfixed by it. For three days each autumn, my work slows and I stare out my south-facing windows at the strange red light pouring through them, until the tree is left, at last, standing naked in a crimson puddle.

In the spring, I watch as each branch leafs out. Some branches don't, and I call the tree man to cut them off, mindful of the day I looked up and saw a huge broken branch suspended above the picnic table and all of my unsuspecting guests.

We have inherited other trees as loved as the maple and that, like it, were planted before we were born. Each spring I stand under the ancient apple, while a white rain of blossoms falls upon my shoulders and the ground, and I am happy, a child again, in a snowstorm… or a boat.

One who plants a garden, plants joy.
— ANCIENT CHINESE PROVERB

23

The Spirit world is connected to
the world of breathing creatures.
An old man can't be too happy about his afterlife.
If his soul should choose a tree after it has left his body,
what will become of it?
What future does a tree have nowadays?

— CHIEF DAN GEORGE, "IF YOUR SOUL SHOULD CHOOSE A TREE"

24

My daughter knows my affection for trees. She brings me spruce and pine seedlings from her summer work of tree-planting and I place them carefully around the yard. A hundred years from now a new owner will wonder why she is living in a forest. "It was planted for love," I would tell her, if I were alive.

The ancient Greeks believed a dryad, a spirit, lived in every tree. And I believe that, too. Certainly the presence of trees makes my yard feel populous. I am tempted to plant a grove of oaks and to lie down in them to meditate, as Druids did, with a stone on my chest to keep me awake. Their novitiate lasted 20 years – two decades of learning, all in the dark oak grove.

That's worth planting oaks for. It's good I am deterred from this by my relative old age, because the flowers I love require more light than can be found beneath an oak.

This is my garden, then. A space in a small city with a medium-sized old house, many borders, a shrinking lawn, and way too many trees. I plant trees to hide the neighbor's air conditioner. Trees to block off the neighbor's dining room window. Trees so I will see leaves and birds from my kitchen window, not an asphalt-covered street.

Indeed, the first thing we did when we moved in was rip up the asphalt parking pad, bring in fresh earth, and plant a new garden right where the black tarry surface had been. Take that! When I can, I will destroy the whole of the remaining driveway, replacing it with gravel so the good rainwater can soak into the ground, instead of running down the road to a storm sewer.

I am at war, in fact. On the one side is *veriditas*, a word invented by the great mystic Hildegarde of Bingen to describe the green energy of growing things. On the other, the powers that pave the earth's surface and then blow salt on it, thinking new highways more important than old farms.

This long struggle goes on all over the world, between the forces that would clear-cut forests and that would bottle the water that is our birthright and sell it back to us – and those who serve *veriditas*.

Every day, I join that battle in my garden. This is why.

Each Thanksgiving, with my grown children home, we hike. We climb a favorite hill outside of town, to a height where we can see the blessed landscape strung out before us. The way up is heavy with fallen poplar and birch leaves, thick and golden, like the streets of heaven.

I relive, then, in my mind, the time the Very Reverend Stan McKay – a Cree holy man and then-leader of my perfectly mainline Protestant church – explained to a little congregation in this city that "This is the holy land." I never tire of this insight. We think the holy land is Jerusalem, and yes, it is lovely, too – golden stone, rich brown hills, a wealth of history.

But this land, to which we are inextricably connected, is also sacred. Therefore, we should tread softly on it, eschew vehicles that tear the soil, ski lightly in winter. This is holy ground.

I plant birch trees in my garden for the gold.

This is the holy land.
– Very Reverend Stan McKay

Interconnectedness. Spirit and body chemistry.
Loving intention. Living with awareness of oneness with
all aspects of life – including each other and food – lies at
the heart of enlightened eating and the mystery of food's
ability to nourish both body and soul. By approaching
food meditatively and with loving intention, we may
go beyond the level of thought and intuit the sacred
connection between Mother Earth, food, and humankind.

– DEBORAH KESTEN, *FEEDING THE BODY, NOURISHING THE SOUL*

GROWING OUR OWN FOOD

My first real garden was in Quebec's Eastern Townships, where there is a long growing season, with a particular lushness seen in the north only at the height of summer. We ambitiously enlarged the little plot behind our house and for several years I played Earth Mother with our children, happily planting rows of vegetables, weeding them, harvesting them, chopping and freezing, pickling and preserving.

In this postmodern world, it couldn't go on. I had a career I thought was important. We are pulled by rugged reality to work in the world of desks and computers, paychecks and telephones.

But there was a wonder about those years, for which I am grateful. In the spring, when the seeds had been planted in rows as straight as we could make them, there was the daily excitement of leaping out of bed and yanking back the curtains to see the little green lines growing stronger and clearer. Beans, peas, carrots, radishes, lettuce, tomatoes, broccoli.

Jim and I each had a parent who had grown up on a farm. We shouldn't have been so astonished that the land could feed us. But we were. And we ate the produce with pleasure, although I confess that after September and October's frenzy of pickling and freezing, I greeted the winter garden with relief.

One day in late summer a friend arrived for dinner and we proudly served up a meal mainly from our garden – carrots,

Be a gardener for Creation.
Dig, toil and sweat, and
turn the earth
upside down,
seek the deepness
and water the plants
in time.
Continue this labor, and
make sweet floods to run,
and noble and abundant
fruits to spring.
Then take this food, drink,
and beauty,
and carry it to God
as your true worship.

— JULIAN OF NORWICH

30

a huge salad, and for the first time, our very own fresh-picked broccoli. Only the chicken legs came from the store.

Soon I noticed that our friend had a small uneaten mound on the side of his plate. He was calmly removing small, green, well-cooked worms from his broccoli, setting them aside without comment. Our children, observing this, did the same and so did Jim and I. "I usually soak the broccoli in salt water before I cook it," he explained comfortably after the meal.

I made a stern internal memo: broccoli, salt, soak, always.

But our friend knew broccoli came from the earth. He didn't use pesticides and (mainly because we didn't know how) neither did we. So he didn't expect perfection. He knew that while the earth feeds us, it also feeds other creatures, some of which may turn up in dinner. We don't own the earth. We simply belong to her and she will feed us as any parent would feed her children.

Each spring, while we lived there, elderly friends would take our two young boys picking fiddleheads. These are very young ferns, still tightly furled, which grow in wet places, such as the oxbow curve of a river. Their locations (like the sites of good blueberry patches in Northern Ontario) are not widely publicized by those who know them. The children, sworn to secrecy, would return home with a proudly conspiratorial air and enormous bags of spring greens.

No one had planted the fiddleheads. They just grew. And they were delicious.

From these amateur efforts at our parents' art (vegetable growing) and from our children's delight in the unmerited fruits of a meandering river, we learned how deeply we belong to the earth. We came to understand that food does not originate in a supermarket freezer. It begins in dirt, soil, land, mud. Even the chicken that accompanied our broccoli at the dinner of the green worms was on our plates only because it had been fed grain grown in earth.

In a small way, there – and sideways, because it hurts to look at it head-on – we began to comprehend the meaning of our species' great power. We humans can alter earth's intricate rhythm of rain and sun. We can destroy the delicate soil-making creatures on which her abundance depends. And then we would be orphaned.

This is why gardening, all gardening, even a pot of geraniums on a balcony, is crucial. It is about connection. We cannot break our time with Mother Earth, or we will starve.

Abundance from Earth

The thing is, earth wants to feed us. We learned that from the tomatoes. We put in exactly 48 plants each year we lived in the Townships. I don't know what was magic about that number, but it was fixed. We staked them as my father had staked his, added manure, and they produced massively.

In late summer, consumed with an emotion I now identify as greed, I would pull the red globes from the stems and pile them on the kitchen counter. I was condemned to hours of making spaghetti sauce (what else can you do with a ton of tomatoes?) but I didn't care. This was abundance.

I had come to understand Eve, you see. The way the story goes…

> When the woman, Eve, saw that the tree was good for food, and that it was a delight to the eyes, and that the tree was to be desired to make one wise, she took of its fruit and ate; and she gave some also to her husband, who was with her, and he ate.

Well, of course. The apple in all its beauty called out to be picked. If exile from Eden is the price to be paid for this glorious greed, so be it. We are called to have knowledge, to grow these fruits well, to learn how to care for the land so that they can continue. It is a gift and Eve knew to take and share it. We learn these lessons of abundance in the garden.

Even today, Eve's delirium at the earth's abundance is at work. My husband rejoices in each fallen leaf – more compost – and drags home bags of manure to layer with it, making a mix as rich as Caesar. This causes the perennials to multiply ferociously. More abundance, which I pass around to friends and strangers.

A woman admired our Siberian iris once. They are dangerous plants, growing larger every year by spreading their long leaves over the ground in winter, killing everything around them. I took her phone number and called her in the spring, when I was dividing them, a task that requires an ax, two shovels, and every muscle in my back.

Fortunately she brought a truck. I watched her drive away feeling a little duplicitous. Those brilliant blue flowers and decorative, graceful leaves would threaten her garden soon enough. But they flourish in the face of salt and sand and drought in the very front of the bed, by the street, and so I love them. Like the tomatoes, and oh yes, the cucumbers (I spent weeks slicing them into pickles), they teach me about the overwhelming, demanding, gorgeous love of God.

It's what all the fruits of the garden teach me. This is a love that places knowledge in our way, offering the chance – which we must pluck for ourselves – to grow up, with all the pain inherent in maturity; to try to re-create Eden. To be generous as earth herself is generous, and to share with one another. To become fit companions for God. I believe the Creator was deeply proud of her rebellious daughter, Eve.

CONNECTED TO BEAUTY, EARTH – AND STRANGERS

Beauty was part of Eden. Eve, discussing disobedience with the serpent, saw clearly that "the tree was good for food, and a delight to the eyes, and that the tree was to be desired to make one wise…"

So I do my best to cultivate beauty for its own sake – a great, addictive pleasure. When we bought our current house in Northern Ontario, it stood in a sea of lawn and asphalt, with a tiny flower bed tucked in one too-shady corner. After many years of rental accommodation, for the first time I had an entirely free hand to do what I wanted.

I was almost paralyzed.

But slowly, I made flower beds, first laying out garden hose to see how each would look, then digging up the grass and tossing the roots onto the compost pile. I piled in well-decayed compost and manure, and then accepted offerings from friends and acquaintances. Because, make no mistake, if you know any

gardeners when you begin a new bed, they will all be joyously at hand with the perennial babies they can't bear to throw away.

At the same time, I read ferociously. (In an earlier gardening career, I had borrowed the then-gardening-Bible, *The Chatelaine Gardening Book*, from the local library so often that they threatened to give it to me.) I dug and read, divided and planted, figuring out which plants needed sun or shade (the most elementary task); what needed to be spirited away from the acidic soil under the big spruce trees; and what could survive in the dry, road-salt-laden, then-treeless front yard.

Making a front flower bed took more than gardening lore. It was an exercise in the relational skills that mark long-lasting marriages. My spouse was deeply uneasy with the radical step of removing grass.

It seems so long ago. I laid out the hose – modestly, so as not to frighten him – and began to dig. A kind man, he rushed to assist. Whenever he wasn't around digging, I quietly eased out the edges, just a tad each time. The completed border was much larger than we had painfully agreed upon.

We added the usual compost and manure, and planted a mix of donated perennials, and annuals left over from a landscaper friend's spring season. Somewhat to our surprise, the garden flourished. Passersby stopped to admire – and my extroverted, conversation-loving spouse became the complete gardener.

The front garden grows larger every year. Although expansion is accompanied even now by groans from my lawn-loving spouse, the affirmation of a flock of strangers has muted his opposition. He is fiercely proud of what our realtor refers to as our home's curb appeal.

In summer, this sunny border is a blaze of Oriental poppies, Shasta daisies, peonies, and Siberian iris (which need water, but love to live so much they'll do without). My spouse loves lilies of every kind. Quick-thinking mutual friends provided huge Oriental lilies on his birthday. The lilies were joined by German iris, Helenium, Michaelmas daisies, flowering raspberry, evening primrose, and masses of day lilies, all tough and prolific.

Early on, my husband told strangers who inquired about the rudbeckia that they were rutabaga. Perhaps they planted accordingly and were puzzled by turnips instead of brilliant yellow sun-faces. But now he knows the name of every plant.

Eve would be proud of me. I disobeyed the iron law decreeing that front yards should consist of lawn, with a few shrubs cowering by the house, and I seduced my husband into doing the same.

And while I was planting that front garden, I planted myself as well. I am rooted and bound now to this yard, on this sometimes busy street, with this crowd of interested passersby, now my friends.

Now more than ever we need to remember that we are vitally connected to the earth. This is not some vague romanticism, but a truth to keep in mind and heart as if our lives depended on it. They do.
— Patrick Lima,
The Organic Home Garden

One day, shopping at the produce store, a stranger came over to me. "What should I do with my roses?" she asked.

I have no idea. I am frightened of roses, all but the hardy shrub roses which will grow no matter what I mistakes I make.

But we talked roses and gardens for a while, there in the store, leaning on our shopping carts, old friends. I didn't even know her name. But we were and are connected to one another through our love of all things green.

Through this, I have discovered that the oneness and unity, the sweet connection with all things we once knew as Eden is not lost at all. It lives here in this small city; in this 21st century; in our postmodern, deconstructionist, cynical world.

Perhaps that little girl, watching the trees slide slowly by from the rowboat, knowing she lived in unity with all of them, would be at home. In our companioned pleasure in the earth we share, in our precious connection to it, gardeners discover paradise.

2

Gardening as Balance

We must cultivate our own garden…
— Voltaire

When I am most wrapped up in the garden, that's just when I must leave it. In spring, say, when flats full of seedlings need hardening off, and weeds need pulling before they get too established, and leaves that were mounded in the fall to protect the front beds from salt need raking off, and early seeds need planting and containers need pulling out of storage to be filled with compost – when my head is full of visions, that's just when I have to pack notebooks and get on the road.

I resist this, but there is no getting around it. Despite Voltaire's dictum, no one gets to live in their garden forever. Life with a garden is a constant balancing of priorities: individual

peace versus the struggle for justice that is more truly paradise. Sometimes the pain of the world seems so agonizing I wonder how I can justify long hours hunched over a perennial bed, pulling out the violets that have multiplied to weeds.

A similar struggle is found in an old Algonquin story.

Once there were two brothers named Glooskap and Malsum, sons of the great Earth Mother. Glooskap was good and wise, while Malsum was evil and selfish. When the Earth Mother died, Glooskap created plants, animals, and humans from her body. Malsum made poisonous plants and snakes and plotted to kill his brother.

One day Malsum told Glooskap he was invincible, except for the roots of a fern plant; he demanded to know what could kill Glooskap. Honest Glooskap confessed he could be killed by an owl feather, so Malsum made a dart from one and killed him.

But the power of good is so strong that Glooskap rose from the dead. Knowing he must protect the creatures he had made, Glooskap lured Malsum to him and flung a fern, pulled out by the roots, at him, killing him.

The struggle between two opposing forces, between retreat from the world and vigorous action, is also found in another old story about brothers, from Hebrew scripture.

Once there were twins named Jacob and Esau. Jacob, born second, was a quiet and skilful farmer. Esau was an equally skilled hunter. On a day when the hunt had been poor, Esau came home starving. Jacob was cooking a rich lentil stew.

"Let me eat some of that red stuff, for I am famished," Esau said.

"First, sell me your birthright," replied Jacob.

Esau said, "I am about to die. What use is a birthright to me?"

"Swear to me first," Jacob said. So Esau swore, and sold his birthright to Jacob. Then Jacob gave Esau bread and lentil stew, and he ate and drank and went his way.

Poor Esau, living so deeply in the moment, so stretched to

A Prayer for May

God of Eden
Give me patience with non-gardeners
Give me words to tell them this is not the time to
phone or visit,
not this month, no.
I am in the garden.

Give me patience, God of all eternity.
It is May. My mind is full of August.
Infant rudbeckia, infant datura;
they'll be tall and filled with bloom.

In due time, patient God, return me to the world
where some garden and some don't.
But not yet.

– Donna Sinclair,
A Woman's Book of Days 2

the limit from the joy of the chase that he would sell his heritage to ease his stomach. And patient, devious Jacob, plotting ahead, lying in wait for the right moment. Cultivation and calm, passion and wilderness. We all carry these rioting currents within. A garden is an attempt to build harmony, to place life into proper proportions, to compensate with order where there is chaos, or to offer a tangle of wilderness where life has grown too rigid.

From the rhythm of light and dark, water and sun, work and rest, the garden teaches balance. It allows Jacob and Esau, Glooskap and Malsum, to co-exist within.

Balancing Technology

Most of us spend our days anchored to the inanimate. After a day of gazing at computer screens, we commute home, regarding the world through a windshield or train window. If we are not careful, we will spend the evening captured by the glowing screen of a television. This is too much framing; our eyes are meant to view a broad horizon. And it's too much artificial light. Our eyes are meant to adjust to sun and shade, starlight and dawn.

For balance, then, it helps to get outside and dig or plant; to weed or prune or deadhead. Life is not framed or ordered for us, out here. Our eyes are busy composing. We wonder, for instance, if that shrub is getting too tall. As an introvert I plant

Nature does have manure and she does have roots as well as blossoms, and you can't hate the manure and blame the roots for not being blossoms.

- BUCKMINSTER FULLER

shrubs to hide behind. Unfortunately, in a few years the garden becomes shaggy, and I attack with the pruning shears.

Pruning during a bad mood stifles timidity. Few shrubs are damaged by strong pruning, at least not the ones I grow: potentilla (which loves to be cut back by about a third each year); spirea (which benefits from severe trimming almost to the ground); honeysuckle (which rapidly takes over my neighbor's driveway, leading to polite but firm remarks about how difficult it is to park the car). Even our lilacs by the door, which need pruning immediately after blooming, are best if they don't endanger the mail carrier's eyes as he strides to our letter box.

But here is what I mean by balance. Computer and television screens never need pruning. They just are, their tidy frames telling us where to look, directing our vision. Such passivity on our part is not good. Life needs us to look around, muse, consider, wander, act.

Similarly, there is balance in deadheading. I go out in the morning to a garden full of spent blossoms. Time is passing, they shout; look at us, dead and gone; winter's coming. It's heartening to travel quickly through the plants, removing all these pessimists. Especially if it is only June.

It's foolish, I know, to think that we can stop time passing. But this activity steadies us in the inexorable world of clocks, which pretend that all time is the same. It isn't. Time is elastic. Days are longer in the spring and shorter in the fall. In June,

We learn from
our gardens
to deal with the most
urgent question of
the time:
how much is enough?

— WENDELL BERRY

[A]rt is nowhere more obvious than in the nice regularities of the potager, its fifty-five or so vegetables ordered by texture and colour and shape. Many different types of lettuces line the edges of the beds; the taller beans and brassicas stand behind; and in the midst are the staked and trellised tomatoes and peas. As the season progresses, the flowering kales and cabbages on the main cross-paths hide the kitchen depredations and broccoli and borecole rise up in place of the earlier summer vegetables.

Are the nasturtiums that line the centre roundel there as insect deterrents, as decoration, or as salad ingredients? Well, all three; and is not the desire to separate these things an index of what is the matter with much gardening — the desire for closure and neatness and discreteness? My mother used to pop tomato plants in behind my father's border roses to his suburban gardener annoyance. But tomatoes were originally thought of as decorative — and why not now?

— DOUGLAS CHAMBER, *STONY GROUND*

we have all the time in the world. In September, we do not. Gardeners own this truth, and it compensates for the suspect wisdom of the workaday world.

SEASONAL BALANCE

Gardens bring harmony between winter and summer, indoors and out: again, a subtle rhythm that is comforting in a too-frantic (and too-often indoors) world. In the spring, I go outside with the baby's tears that have dotted my rooms with green for months. I shake them out of their pots and plant them in rich soil in deep shade. They spread there making that area of the garden gentle and soft. These are well-named plants.

In the fall, before the first hint of frost (again well-named, baby's tears are very tender) I dig them up and pot them for the house. By now, many pots are required. I take them inside and forget them, except for regular watering, in the basement windows. In early January, when the house seems dull and bare, I give some away, and bring the rest upstairs, where they spill joyously over the edges of their pots, compensating for the solemn post-Christmas house.

I love this seasonal drift from house to land and back again. I learn patience in it. For every time of energy and growth, there is a time of sleep, stillness, and perhaps sadness. This is the way the world is. Even now, I look out my window and see the wooden lawn chairs, huddled conversationally in a semicircle,

Speak to the earth, and
it shall teach thee.
— BIBLICAL PROVERB

patiently awaiting habitation. We have no room to store them indoors and thus they need frequent painting. But we love them, expectant and snow-laden, promising the exhilaration of the spring.

Brothers in the Soul

Jacob knew patience. Esau was a skilful hunter, a man of the field, while Jacob was a quiet man, living in tents. Gardeners should consider Jacob, who waited until the right moment and bought his brother's heritage with a bowl of lentils. Jacob later cheated Esau of their father's blessing, and fled to the land of his uncle Laban. There he waited seven years for the hand of the woman he loved. Tricked into marrying her sister, he waited another seven so he could have both. Marriage arrangements were more flexible at the time.

Finally, Jacob embarked on a careful, slow breeding program that produced strong sheep and goats. He grew wealthy and headed home. But – almost there – he spent a long night wrestling with a shadowy figure: God, an angel, a river daemon, his own soul, his shadow… there are many interpretations. And then, despite his well-founded fears of reprisal, the wounded, limping Jacob was reconciled with the brother he had wronged. Esau ran to meet him, the story says, and embraced him, and fell on his neck and kissed him and they wept.

In the same way, Jacob and Esau need to be reconciled within us. We don't want to be stealing another's birthright. Wise gardeners live as lightly on the land as hunters.

In his very beautiful *Jacob's Wound,* Trevor Herriot argues that the story of Jacob and Esau, farmer and hunter, is "a powerful myth that traces the path we took in forsaking our original lifeways and driving out our wilder, pre-agricultural brethren." The beginning of agriculture was also the beginning of riches and accumulation and fences and high walls. We discovered that "betrayal, subjugation, and disenfranchisement leave us wounded, longing to be blessed, and in need of a new identity that will place us once more in the presence of God as we knew it in Eden."

Because the garden of Creation belongs to all. Those who store up riches (like Jacob) and those who leave no footprint (like Esau) co-exist on a planet that the former has endangered far more than the latter.

Gardeners know that their own land does not exist in isolation from others. I am alert, in my own small piece of land, for the effects of a smelter about 120 kilometers away. New scrubbers ease the problem greatly; but a superstack still spreads sulphur dioxide thinly over many acres. So I watch the acidity of the soil. When moss threatens to take over the back yard completely (even though I love its softness) we add lime or fireplace ash. When the maple loses another branch, I check, worried, for die-back at the crown.

That's simple enough. The clash between technology and people of the land is harsher in many places. In Iraq, for instance, under American occupation as I write, the economy has been reorganized to give control to large global corporations. Under Order 81 (concerning patents) the 10,000-year-old practice of saving and exchanging their own seeds has become illegal. The only seeds Iraqi farmers are supposed to plant are "protected" varieties owned by large agricultural companies, which are guaranteed a large profit.

This land, now called Iraq, was once the fertile crescent in which people first began to set aside seed from plants that bore well, replanting them year by year. This was the cradle

PRAYER FOR OCTOBER

Fruitful God,
we praise thee
for the summer that was,
the blooming, and the
pleasant work,
the resting in the shade.
Healing God,
we praise thee for
the snowfalls and the
bookish days
the resting by the fire.
Glorious is thy world,
O God,
and we in it, blessed;
glorious is thy world.

— DONNA SINCLAIR

A WOMAN'S BOOK OF DAYS 2

of agriculture. And these policies set in place by an occupying power represent the desire for wealth gone wildly out of balance.

LOCAL EDEN

As gardeners, we deal first with our own land. We make our compost, grow tough native plants, water as little as we can.

This is harder than it looks. I love a strip of green next to our street, for instance, where the soil is thin and hard, and everything is killed each winter by salty run-off. For many years we re-sodded this piece annually, to the neighbors' amusement, and poured on the water.

But prodded by conscience, and our city's sensible encouragement to save water, we learned to plant a tough cottage mix of rye and clover on that strip instead. We carefully arranged boxes of freshly pulled weeds on it – proof of ongoing labor – to discourage parking until it was solid ground cover. Although this effort is on municipal property, our neighbors graciously indulge us, and our precious green survives.

We bought a rain barrel, which we use for water-hungry containers on the driveway as much as possible. Borders fend for themselves, except for selective watering of new young annuals and very thirsty plants, which we do meditatively with handheld hose.

We save seeds, as well as buy them.

Because we don't use pesticides, the hosta are full of toothy holes, and the starry pink blossoms of the Nelly Moser clematis last only a day before earwigs reduce them to lace.

We don't mind.

We know, because we are in the garden decade after decade, that the climate is changing. We try, slowly and not well, to change our long-established wasteful ways. We may even have to step out of the garden sometimes, protesting those who would make war. War is bad for gardens and for those who till them.

What we are about is resisting overcivilization, even in ourselves. We can try to protect the birthrights of others. Especially now, when so much is straight lines of highways, engineered hills, and angular cement buildings that crowd out the sun. We can preserve the opposite, the little creatures of the soil, a tangle of brush for the birds, flowers, trees.

We can be like Glooskap, saving the world with a fern root. Or like Esau, who said to Jacob in the end, "Let us journey on our way, and I will go alongside you."

3

Gardening as Memory

Once the earth and the sky were very close. From their great love, Rangi (Father Sky) and Papatuanuku (Mother Earth) came their seventy children, the gods. But there was no room for the gods to grow, because the earth and sky were pressed so close.

Finally Tane-mahuta, the gentle god of the forest, stood on his head and pushed up with his legs, straight up, as a tree grows. With his shoulders on Papatuanuku and his feet on Rangi, he pushed and pushed them apart, while his parents screamed and groaned.

But now there was space. Light and dark were separated, the gods had room,

tall trees grew and humans and animals thrived.

Rangi is still sad to be separated from Papatuanuku, though. His tears form the morning dew, and the rain.

— A POLYNESIAN STORY

When my husband accepted a job in a large metropolis, almost 300 kilometers away from our home, it felt like exile. Like many couples, over the course of our marriage we had moved frequently and I had learned to pull up stakes willingly, or, when it was my turn to make the decision, to refuse. "I'd like to move here," I would say cheerfully, indicating our current home. Sometimes I would offer to put all our furniture on the front lawn and then bring it back in.

The story of Rangi and Papatuanuku tells it well. Gardeners don't like to be separated from the land. But sometimes it is necessary to allow some space between us and the land we love, in order for good things to happen. So this time, we agreed. We would go. It was a matter of vocation, of challenge, of maturity and growth. Our new home, we decided, would be in Toronto. Our present house in Northern Ontario would become the cottage.

"There," we said, after several weeks of agonized discussion, "that wasn't hard!" I would live most of the time at the now-cottage; he would come home (to the cottage) on weekends. I would spend one week each month in the city.

We found a tiny apartment, downtown, with a balcony facing south, surrounded by a great deal more concrete than I like. *Cimento es progreso*, we muttered to one another, echoing slogans we had seen painted on walls in Latin America. Cement is progress.

Sure.

And then the strangest thing happened. I found myself bringing clay pots up 11 stories and lugging them onto the balcony. I piled the car with bags of Jim's good compost. Soon I was transporting a few flats of the seedlings I had started for what I was starting to think of as "the big garden" back home. The balcony had become our "Toronto garden," and I set to work with as much vigor and even joy as if it was an acre of land instead of a shelf of concrete. It was as Rangi and Papatuanuku had discovered. Sometimes a new space simply allows people to thrive.

At the same time, however, I understood that this was a form of exile and that I was simply doing as a wise man named Jeremiah had ordered, in another illuminating story.

Once there was a great prophet named Jeremiah. After the people of Israel were taken into captivity in Babylon (598 BCE) Jeremiah wrote a letter to the elders in exile, words of hope that he had received from God:

We are only visitors here in this part of Creation, We are guests of the one who owns this Creation. We are always to keep in mind that we can own nothing here, not even our own lives. So the purpose of life then is not to acquire possessions but to honour the Creator by how we live.
— ARTHUR SOLOMON,
THERE IS NO MIDDLE GROUND

> Thus says the LORD of hosts, the God of Israel, to all the exiles... Build houses and live in them, plant gardens and eat what they produce. ...seek the welfare of the city where I have sent you into exile, and pray to the LORD on its behalf, for in its welfare you will find your welfare.
>
> – JEREMIAH 29:4–7 RETOLD

To my own astonishment, I was following the prophet's advice. I was as happy puttering on that balcony as I was in what now seemed our enormous acreage up north. I found ways to keep the soil moist during the weeks when we were absent and soon we had a bumper crop of basil, along with masses of drought-resistant rudbeckia, African daisies, and marigolds. We could sit outside in the summer evening and smell the rich herbs as we brushed against them, which – given our balcony's small size – was often.

Still, I wondered. I was supposed to be cranky, missing the land. But I was perfectly content: exiled, but at home.

Then I heard a radio interview with a scientist named Douglas Larson. He and four colleagues at the University of Guelph had come up with a theory that our ancestors of a million years ago were cliff dwellers. Climate change had forced them out of the forests and onto the savannas; and from there they had made their way to the shelter of caves and cliffs.

Everyone has enough weeding to do in their own garden.
– FLEMISH PROVERB

After the first 600,000 years they discovered fire and found ways to use the tough plants and animals they found there. For the next 460,000 years, they lived off the resources of the nearby savannas and riverbank forests, but stayed on in their caves at the cliff-bases. When they finally ventured forth, between 30,000 and 12,000 years ago, they simply re-created many of the features of their rocky home wherever they went. "Certain configurations of the built environment have always made us feel comfortable and safe. Huts, houses, castles, and skyscraping towers all have the feel of home because each of them has features of the original paradise," says Larson in his book *The Urban Cliff Revolution*. "The idea of cities as safe homes might explain why people around the world continue to flock there when economic difficulties arise."

Out of deep memory, perhaps, I was doing what our earliest ancestors had done. I had found a safe place high on a rocky cliff (apartment building) and some tough opportunistic species to share it with. Perhaps my choice of plants wasn't entirely authentic. According to Lawson's Cliff Ecology Research Group, cabbage and carrots and rice are among the refugees from the talus slopes that accompanied the exodus. When early humans ventured away from the sheltering rocks, they took their seeds with them and watched them flourish in a richer environment.

The Seven of Pentacles

Under a sky the color of
pea soup
she is looking at her work
growing away there
actively, thickly like
grapevines or pole beans
as things grow in the real
world, slowly enough.
If you tend them properly,
if you mulch, if you water,
if you provide birds that
eat insects a home and
winter food,
if the sun shines and you
pick off caterpillars,
if the praying mantis comes
and the ladybugs and
the bees,
then the plants flourish, but
at their own internal clock.
Connections are made
slowly, sometimes they
grow underground.
You cannot tell always by

looking what is happening.
More than half the tree is
spread out in
the soil under your feet.
Penetrate quietly as
the earthworm that
blows no trumpet.
Fight persistently as the
creeper that brings
down the tree.
Spread like the squash
plant that overruns
the garden.
Gnaw in the dark and use
the sun to make sugar.

Weave real connections,
create real nodes,
build real houses.
Live a life you can endure:
Make love that is loving.
Keep tangling and
interweaving and
taking more in,

a thicket and bramble
wilderness to the outside
but to us
interconnected with
rabbit runs and
burrows and lairs.

Live as if
you liked yourself, and
it may happen: reach out,
keep reaching out,
keep bringing in.
This is how we are going to
live for a long time:
not always,
for every gardener knows
that after the digging,
after the planting,
after the long season of
tending and growth,
the harvest comes.

– Marge Piercy

67

*If we do not permit
the Earth to produce
beauty and joy,
it will in the end not
produce food either.*
– Joseph Wood Krutch

Fellow Exiles

With the balcony came rock doves, or pigeons we call them. According to Larson and his colleagues, they had migrated – along with dogs and cockroaches and rats and lice – and set up shop in the new cliffs humans obligingly built. This would explain the anguish of the birds I tried to discourage from nesting in my spring-planted pansies. They were sure this was their cliff, not mine. It became outright war. They laid eggs in the clay pots and desecrated the floor. Terribly. Only seagulls can rival the amount of guano a pigeon can lay down in a day.

We won the battle by deploying netting. Our balcony resembles the well-meshed American embassy in El Salvador, ready to repel rockets. Or pigeons. The flowers continued to grow wildly, poking out through the net barrier as if it didn't exist. The pigeons went on to less-protected spaces, although the occasional feather still floats through. I installed wicker chairs and a sisal rug, and gazed with pleasure at the city below, secure in my 21st-century cave and a million years of memory.

Memory and Myth

In fact, I was enchanted with the whole idea of cliff-dwelling humans and plants. When I began to think of the concrete as cliff rock – instead of the result of quarrying – I felt more accepting. The fact I could see trees below helped as well. I began to enjoy the urban forest, dreaming of Tane-mahuta, keeping the earth and sky apart.

I already knew, of course, how gardens hold memory: the plants given by faraway friends; the spirit of my father whispering the name of a puzzling weed.

Some garden memories are not even entirely real. The garden that surrounds my house, for instance, is a traditional English country garden. A cottage garden. The fact that such a garden never really existed is beside the point. "The truth is," says garden historian Roy Strong, in his book *Small Period Gardens*, "the cottage garden of our imagination is as artificial a creation as the most formal and grand of the large gardens, and those who set out to plant a cottage garden are not so much recreating a lost reality as making real the rose-tinted vision of a school of water-colour painters…"

Planting perennial beds with layers of color, tucking trailing plants to fall loosely over containers, I have been creating a myth. The story my garden tells goes roughly like this.

Once upon a time, before the invention of plastic, people had a powerful innate sense of beauty that is now compromised. What's natural is best. Slugs and earwigs are part of the landscape. Every garden should have old roses and phlox. We must preserve our heritage.

This may be fiction, but I'll stand by it. And I try to insert, where I can, aspects of a true cottage garden, which would have

Gardeners, like everyone else, live second by second and minute by minute. What we see at one particular moment is then and there before us. But there is a second way of seeing. Seeing with the eye of memory, not the eye of our anatomy, calls up days and seasons past and years gone by.
– ALLEN LACY,
THE GARDENER'S EYE

contained many vegetables and herbs. Such gardens would have had a pig and chickens, too. I believe my family and neighbors are grateful for city bylaws prohibiting this.

So I am contented with foxgloves and calendula, borage and bee balm, shrub roses and sage, because the story this garden tells, the mythic memory it evokes, is good. (If I could keep bees as well – also not allowed – I would.) We need a vision of nature loved, of pesticide-free plants, of integration and wholeness and co-existence – an alternative to a culture too much taken with efficiency over beauty.

Cottage gardens are not efficient. They require transplanting and weeding, constant deadheading and pruning. But they are soft in a hard world. Their generous plantings and old-world feel touch the heart, a muscle too-long secondary to the head.

Further, they *do* have a legitimate basis in the small plots that held laborers' cottages during the early 19th century – the very cottages from which my own paternal ancestors sprung. These working people eked out their diet with homegrown vegetables and berries, a tradition my own grandparents continued when they emigrated to North America.

"Build houses and live in them, plant gardens and eat what they produce…seek the welfare of the city where I have sent you into exile," said Jeremiah. I am the grandchild of those who left the land they loved, for my sake. Even idealized, this garden is my own.

Ancestors in the Garden

As well as a place of alternate vision – or myths – my garden is peopled with wise ones, living and dead. They are with me in spirit. It's a phrase hackneyed from overuse, but rich and true anyway.

My father is an omnipresent spirit in my garden. Before his death, I lived with spouse and children in a pleasant bungalow, not our own, with a small yard. Although I had been Earth Mother herself before moving in, here I kept only a few halfhearted barrels of geraniums by the front walk.

Perhaps I was mourning the array of beans and tomatoes, carrots and peas, all surrounded by the swaying white and purple cosmos of our previous garden. In any case, Grandpa and Grandma were now only two hours away by car. The children weren't picking carrots in their own backyard, but there was always Grandpa's. It was jammed with sweet carrots, and peas on the vine, and raspberry canes so well-pruned and tended that small children could sit under them and eat the fat red fruit with little fear of thorns.

To dig in one's own earth,
with one's own spade,
does life hold
anything better?
– Beverly Nichols

And then one November Grandpa died. The tools had been cleaned and put away for the winter and the parsnips stored in the cool cellar. It was a gardener's death – everything tidy and the tulips in the ground ready to herald his belief, next spring, in the resurrection.

That May I drove to my mother's to put a few petunias in the bed by the front steps. The tulips were already marching in a blaze of color the full length of the backyard. The perennials, I knew, were well-weeded and newly divided, and would carry on with help from someone we could hire. I headed for my father's compost pile, to give the transplanted petunias a good start.

It was magnificent compost. Three sections, carefully fenced: one for new clippings and weeds; one in the middle, semi-decayed, with solid lashings of manure; the last well-rotted and ready to use. I dug into the third and I could feel my father's steady presence.

The next day I drove home with a large bag of his compost in the back of the car. That summer the geraniums in my token front-yard barrels exploded, the petunias accompanying them threatening to take over the sidewalk.

And suddenly, I wanted to garden again. I came out of mourning. We bought our current house the next year, with its large yard, my father silently approving. His spirit has been here ever since, taking pleasure in the expanding beds, the proliferation of trees, the new lilacs, the experiments with pots, the rain barrel, and most of all, in his much-loved son-in-law's compost heap, rich and brown and crumbly, which underpins it all.

SPIRITS IN THE GARDEN

There are others here besides my father. My grandfather hovers near the peony he gave me years ago from his own garden. I have moved it everywhere, even to the house-without-a-garden.

Friends, rejoicing at our happiness, have brought offerings from their own gardens, and I think of them often.

My brother sent a matchbox of tiny brown "bulblets" in the mail. They were from lilies taken years before from our father's garden. Each summer they form a fiery red clump, and I think of my father and my brother.

And sometimes, in my garden, I think of John Cree. I don't know him well. I interviewed him in 1990, during the Oka crisis, as the world called it, when Kanesatake and Kahnawake, in Quebec, exploded into a standoff between Mohawk warriors, police, and army. Cree is the elder who had led the morning prayers and sprinkled tobacco on a tiny fire marking a roadblock – the attempt by the people of the pines to prevent the trees from being cleared for a golf course.

I won't forget that interview. I was hyper. All the journalists were hyper, because we were in the middle of a story that had brought film crews and reporters from around the world. John Cree had graciously invited me into his home, and I clutched

Because we don't think about future generations, they will never forget us.
– HENRIK TIKKANEN

75

my notebook and fired questions at him: how many guns, how many warriors?

He didn't answer right away. Instead, he offered me an apple – precious, with the now-massive blockade in progress – because he is hospitable and perhaps because munching kept me occupied so he could speak. He began to talk slowly and deliberately about those prayers, that morning by the fire, and about the acknowledgment and gratitude they contained for all the creatures of this earth, starting with the little bugs and worms that give health to the soil.

This took a long time. I grew calm, which also may have been his intent. Then we talked quietly about the siege and what it cost the community; we talked about the frustration and idealism and rage of the warriors, about the courage of the women. I wrote my story, and a few other stories as well. Eventually the siege at Oka ended and the reporters, like me, went home.

But a piece of that spirit stays with me. Because of John Cree's presence, I cannot harm the small creatures of the soil. Because of the warriors' guarding of the pines, I cannot see the land as less than sacred.

Gardens are about memory. They help us remember the good given to us by the Creator.

History and Hope

It is not given to any people to stay in one place forever. We have only to think of Rangi and Papatuanuku, or of Jeremiah's people driven into Babylonian exile, aching for home. Or of our own grandparents – or of ourselves – coming to this land in the great waves of immigration that continue to this day.

But we make our homes where we are. Jeremiah's advice is still good. "Build houses and live in them, plant gardens and eat what they produce."

As the prophet explains a little later in his letter to the exiles, God has promised that captivity will end. "For surely I know the plans I have for you, says the LORD, plans for your welfare and not for harm, to give you a future with hope." And someday "again, you will plant vineyards on the mountains of Samaria; the planters shall plant and enjoy the fruit…"

I cling to these words, not because I yearn for Samaria; but because as a gardener I exist simultaneously at home and in exile. In the space around my home, I imagine the whole earth without any soil drenched with dioxin; with no toxic salt spray thrown up from the road; with an ozone layer that has not grown thin, allowing fragile seedlings to burn and twist in the sun – an earth where, as God promised Jeremiah, "life shall become like a watered garden."

That is our true home. And we are all in exile from it, as long as suburbs sprout on fine land good for precious crops; or farmers on any continent must leave their land to live.

So gardeners – in the line of Jeremiah, the prophet – watch the sun and the rain and talk of global warming. And then we make a little paradise, a little watered garden, so that those who stop and wonder at the bustling plants will remember how it was. We cannot rest. But God has promised. The exile cannot last forever.

If a healthy soil is
full of death, it is also
full of life: worms, fungi,
microorganisms of all
kinds ...
Given only
the health of the soil,
nothing that dies is
dead for very long.
— WENDELL BERRY,
THE UNSETTLING OF AMERICA, 1977

4

Gardening as Healing

Calendula is the mainstay of any good homeopathic first aid kit, and can be used on all minor cuts, grazes, shallow wounds, and scalds.

– Cassandra Marks in *Homeopathy: A Step-by-Step Guide*

Time in the garden makes you feel better. A multitude of plants make useful cures. These are not surprises to a gardener. A story, retold from the Chippewa and Algonquin, bears this out.

Once, not long after the world was made, humans and animals could talk with one another. But humans began to kill the trusting animals for clothing and food, and they became angry. The bears decided to make war on humans, but couldn't throw a spear or shoot arrows because of their claws.

GARDENING IS A GOOD FORM OF EXERCISE

As with most exercise programs, the activity must be maintained for a period of a least 30 minutes to be beneficial.

Burn calories, lose weight
(calories burned per half hour)
- Digging and spading: women burn 150 calories, men 197
- Cutting grass with a power rotary mower: women burn 135 calories, men 177
- Weeding flower beds/vegetable garden: women burn 138 calories, men 181
- Digging and shoveling: burn 250 to 350 calories
- Turning compost: burn 250 to 300 calories

Overall health
Recent research indicates that 30 minutes daily of moderate exercise, such as gardening,
- lowers blood pressure and cholesterol levels
- helps prevent diabetes
- prevents or slows osteoporosis.

The deer chose not to make war, but magic. If a hunter killed a deer and forgot to ask permission first – or seek pardon afterward – he or she would soon have rheumatism.

The fish and reptiles decided to haunt humans with terrible dreams, which only the Cherokee can banish, and only with the help of a medicine person. The birds and insects met and each named a different disease they could spread among the humans.

The plants, however, felt the animals were too harsh in their judgment, since many of them also killed for food. Since they overheard all these decisions, they knew exactly what diseases were coming. Each plant decided to act as a cure for one disease. And that was the beginning of medicine.

Gardens are therapeutic in many ways. I dimly remember the railway gardens from my childhood. My father worked for the Temiskaming and Northern Ontario Railway, later the Ontario Northland Railway. So we traveled by train; in fact, my parents didn't own a car until long after I had left home. At every station where we stopped and started and shunted and eventually moved on, there was a garden – a sudden, incongruous slash of color before we re-entered a landscape of endless trees.

I didn't think to question this. I had never known anything else. Railroads had been encouraging gardening around the stations and their employees' homes since long before I was born. Thumbing through a history book in the library, I found a black and white photo of a greenhouse and generous perennial beds adjacent to the T&NO railway station at Englehart, 1917. "Such greenhouses supplied the annuals so necessary for the typical railway garden," says garden historian Edwinna von Baeyer in her book *Rhetoric and Roses*.

I was charmed. That's where I grew up, and my mother before me. I asked her about it. "Oh yes," she said. "I used to play with the gardener's daughter." 1917: she would have been four years old.

What I hadn't known was that the Canadian Pacific Railway had been "Canada's head gardener," according to von Baeyer. For almost 70 years, until railway passenger travel dimmed under the onslaught of planes and cars in the 1960s, the CPR was actively designing beds, supplying seeds and plants, hiring gardeners, and maintaining nurseries, with its own Forestry Department to keep it all going. At its peak, says von Baeyer, the company oversaw "gardens dotted along 25,749 km of track, from coast to coast, through every climatic condition possible in Canada."

Other railways, like the T&NO which employed my father, followed suit. It was good public relations. It persuaded would-be

settlers that the land was fertile (even though in some northern sections the soil was so thin more had to be brought in).

Most of all, though, employers believed that gardening was good for their workers. Von Baeyer quotes the *Canadian Municipal Journal* from 1908.

> The man with a nice garden is not the man who has to be discharged for beating his wife and neglecting his children. The man with a nice garden is a decent industrious man, who will bring up his children to be the best kind of citizens.

It's a striking (if paternalistic) example of an early employee assistance program. An employee with an anger management problem today would be sent to a therapist; and it's doubtful that any company would feel free to step in if he or she was neglecting the children (although a good employee plan would offer them a therapist, too).

This faith in the healing properties of working with earth is appealing. Somewhere in our rush from the land to the city, we lost it. I wish we could have it back. It's all found in this story, retold from John's gospel.

> Once when Jesus was walking along with his disciples, they saw a man blind from birth. The disciples wondered if some sin of his or of his parents had caused this. "Neither," said Jesus, although he explained that God's works would be revealed in him.

Then Jesus spat on the ground and made mud, and spread the mud on the man's eyes, and told him to go and wash in the pool of Siloam.

He went and washed and came back able to see.

It's an echo of the account in Genesis and other creation stories. The Creator breathes on a handful of earth to create a human being. Jesus spits on a handful of earth, and heals with it. If we are wise, we, too, will play with earth and mud, and be healed.

Healing from What?

Before healing, there is a question. What ails us? The Victorians who decreed that good employees should produce a garden believed in original sin (a notion many of us have discarded in favor of original blessing). Decent living and loyal toil kept sinners from harm, and also suited their employers greatly. Gardens were to heal this fallen state, or at least mitigate it.

But we are not born sinners, we declare today. We are born blessed by the love of God and by creation's beauty. We have learned from the Celts, who migrated here in large numbers from Scotland and Ireland, that creation is sacred, a gift to all of us. As one Celtic prayer says:

Thanks be to thee, Jesu Christ

For the many gifts thou hast bestowed upon me,

Each day and each night, Each sea and each land,

Each weather fair, each calm, each wild.

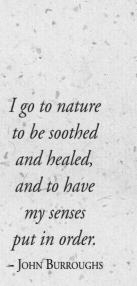

I go to nature to be soothed and healed, and to have my senses put in order.

– John Burroughs

*There is always Music
amongst the trees
in the Garden,
but our hearts must be
very quiet to hear it.*

— MINNIE AUMONIER

What ails us today is not our fallen state, but our separation from the physical world, from "common Creation," in the words of Celtic expert Esther de Waal – a creation in which humans are not a separate order of being. They are simply much-loved creatures of God, like the deer and the wolf, the birds and the small beetles that labor constantly to keep the soil sweet.

De Waal retells the legend of Cuthbert, the Celtic saint who walked barefoot, praying, for hours on the shore of the bitterly cold North Sea, while two small otters played around his feet, "warming them with their breath and trying to dry them with their fur."

This was not a man playing with his pets, she explains. It was a vision of a man so transfigured in prayer that "the right order of Creation" was restored.

We need healing from a world that tears us away from that right order. And that's what gardens provide. In a world of sensory overload, with too much noise and too much harsh light, gardens offer a certain silence, a quality of light, smell, texture, and color. In the garden we step away from e-mail and ringing phones; not quite back a century, that's not possible for 21st-century minds. But we can reach for what climate change, noise and light pollution try to steal from us: the rightful rhythm of sun and shade, the healing touch of sun on skin, night with darkness and starlight, and morning birdsong.

The Healing Garden: Silence

The notion of the healing garden is pleasant, but not easy to create. We can only attempt to get close to it.

First, sound is important. Most of us live with electronic noise: the radio waking us up, the beep of the microwave at breakfast, the phone, the doorbell, the car radio, the alarm we accidentally set off when we open our vehicle, the little *harrumphs* of our computers trying to get our attention, the various peals of cell phones (our own and others'), the car radio again, the television, sirens, air conditioners.

That is why I like the early-morning garden. It's quiet, except for crows, who make a raucous clamor at certain times. But that's creature noise. Children playing is very good noise – they're creatures, too – while someone's radio tuned to a station with a lot of revved-up commercials is not.

Achieving peace in the garden takes work: thick cedars planted to screen a neighboring air conditioner, trees and shrubs in the front yard for leaf sound against the traffic. Careful conversations about outside radios can help, if you stay civil and be a good neighbor.

If I weren't worried about roots clogging up our water pipes, I would plant a grove of trembling aspen. When traffic is heavy past my front door, I still pause and think about the way the slightest breeze makes them clatter so they drown all other sound.

This is not – I repeat – an attempt to step back in time. It is an effort to hear the sound of earth. It is no accident, however, that those who lived a long time ago heard that sound clearly and knew what it was. As a poem dated 806 CE says,

Melodious music the birds perform
to the King of the heaven of the clouds,
Praising the radiant King
Hark from afar the choir of the birds.

Beauty

Silence heals. And so does beauty. Not only our ears but our eyes can be assaulted as we go about our day. A dose of loveliness, like an aspirin a day or some extra vitamin C, may be good for the heart. Andrew Weil, in a charming, hopeful, possibly fictitious book called *8 Weeks to Optimum Health* suggests we buy fresh flowers as part of our health regimen. I read that and trusted him at once.

It's hard to be persuasive about this, because much of the world prizes commerce over beauty. And our notions about what precisely constitutes beauty vary from one person to another.

Still. We have to start somewhere. Here are some ideas.

Because I believe in the sheer goodness of creation, I lean toward the natural as beautiful. Those railway gardens I saw from the train window in the 1940s, with their masses of

*Always remember
the beauty of
the garden,
for there is peace.*
– Author Unknown

*"All the beings of the world
pray," said my Grandad...
"Each living thing gives its
life to the beauty of all life,
and that gift is its prayer."*
– Douglas Wood,
Grandad's Prayers of the Earth

The real voyage of discovery consists not in seeking new landscapes but in having new eyes.

— MARCEL PROUST

carefully arranged annuals, probably wouldn't please me now, although I would like them better than the asphalt that often replaces them.

Of course, my own garden isn't really natural either. If it were, I would let the violets take over as they wish and I wouldn't struggle with the orange day lilies that are as indestructible as concrete. My garden only *pretends* to be natural, with drifts of flowers repeated at intervals to balance the bed, the taller ones generally in the middle because my beds are seen from both sides.

I divide perennials in the fall so that each plant comes up looking whole in the spring; I tuck in annual plants and seeds around them, and let some self-sowers thrive. The California poppies, for instance. Put them in one year and you have them forever – wonderful golden drops of color that fling themselves all over a sunny bed and take your breath away. Photographers who wait until evening, to avoid harsh light in their photos, arrive at my garden to find the poppies closed, thin pencils of gold. Nothing I can do will persuade them to open when the sky is overcast or the day is shutting down.

I have to be blunt with the evening primrose, which lace themselves everywhere, arriving, I think, in the compost. Which leads to another remark about the beauty issue. Color. Certain plants have a place in my garden because someone I love gave them to me. But sometimes the colors clash horribly.

*Never lose an opportunity
of seeing anything that is
beautiful,
for beauty is God's
handwriting — a wayside
sacrament.
Welcome it in every fair
face, in every fair sky, in
every flower,
and thank God for it as a
cup of blessing.*

— RALPH WALDO EMERSON

The bright yellow of the evening primrose is too hot. And the Oriental poppies, which my spouse loves, I leave untouched although they multiply spectacularly. We spent many summers wandering along the front bed, counting the new whorls of dark green leaves and smiling. Little did we know. Unfortunately their color ranges from salmon to orange. If the peonies happen to bloom at the same time, and odds are they will, various shades of pink get added to the mix. Every year I mutter about marking the offending colors with thread, so I can move them apart after blooming, and every year I forget. Planting shrubs seems to help. The green background cools the violence.

Perhaps the person who invented stand-alone signs with huge neon letters felt the same way. Maybe he or she fell in love with the garish colors. I don't know. They are surpassingly ugly, though. Those signs, and orange street lights, and massive parking lots coated in black and butting up hard against the wall of a plantless building, and rusty chain link fences – those are why we need gardens. Something to rest our eyes.

Rhythm in the Garden

The garden heals because it has a rhythm to it, like a mother's heartbeat. I can't change that rhythm, no matter how perfectionist and controlling I feel. It shakes me, smooths me, forces me away from self-willed compulsion and into a kind of deference to the earth.

*Every spring is
the only spring —
a perpetual astonishment.*
– ELLIS PETERS

*Gardens were before
gardeners, and but some
hours after the earth.*

– Sir Thomas Browne

That probably reads as impossibly mystical. Just the kind of thing a person who thought it was a great idea to smear mud on someone's eyes would write. But the thing is, the garden does help me see. It gives me new eyes.

During any gardening day, I move from sun to shade and back again. Against all advice, I seldom wear sunscreen, preferring to absorb vitamin D while I can. But I move into a shady area to work as soon as I am hot. When I am cool, I move back out into the sun. Each time I do that, things look different.

In the same way, I move through a gardening day alternating between working and resting. When it stops being fun, I pause, read a book, have a coffee, lie in the shade. Pause time. Wasted time. It's a concept not well known in our other lives as workers. Hammocks belong to gardens for a reason.

And then there's the night-and-day rhythm for a gardener, perfectly suited to what we do, with the long days of early summer (just when we have quantities of tasks), to the shortening days of autumn (when we wait – almost impatiently – for the first touch of frost to make it okay to start emptying pots). This ordered elasticity of time is imposed upon us. We cannot will more daylight, and gardening under a streetlight, while possible, is not as sweet.

And the seasons, the long rhythm of the year, tune us to the beat of our ancestors, offering a gentle counterpoint to everydayness. Now we work and now we clean our tools and now we hibernate and build fires.

All of this is considered, ordered and arranged. As Celtic poet George F. MacLeod said,

Almighty God, Creator:
The morning is Yours, rising into fullness.
The summer is Yours, dipping into autumn.
Eternity is Yours, dipping into time.
The vibrant grasses, the scent of flowers,
the lichen on the rocks, the tang of seaweed.
All are Yours.
Gladly we live in this garden of Your creating.

SEEING MORE CLEARLY

About a block below our house was a railway line. Just lately the tracks were ripped up. We can walk along it now, a trail in the middle of the city surrounded on both sides by thick bush.

For an acre or so along this line, Mr. Sweetman has planted a garden. His house is nearby and his own garden spilled over into this one years ago. It is reminiscent of the railway gardens, but more naturalized. He plants perennials where railway employees clung stubbornly to annuals (even as railroad executives pleaded with them for more natural beauty and less expense).

Over many years of gardening, Mr. Sweetman has divided the perennials over and over, creating a glorious, idiosyncratic panorama of rocky paths and ponds and streams with huge iris and lily beds, daisies and phlox, roses and lilacs. Some plants he rescued from the garbage. In fact, the area was once a dump.

Now people come for wedding photos, or picnics, or just to walk. Every gardener in the city says from time to time, "Let's go see what's blooming now in Mr. Sweetman's garden."

He used to be a teacher. That's why he is always "Mr." Sweetman.

And he teaches us still, about beauty. About how one man's singular obsession can destroy ugliness. About long life and community and seeing beauty where there was none before.

That's how it worked with the blind man Jesus met. A little mud, a little earth, and things are seen more clearly. We are healed.

5

Gardening as Hope

Once, in the days when the Ojibway lived by hunting and fishing, a hard existence, a young man with the power of shamanic visions went to the forest to fast. He prayed for a spirit guide, to help him end the people's hunger.

The spirit guide came dressed in green and yellow with a green feather headdress, and said, "Wrestle with me." Even though the young man was weak with hunger, he did so, and they did this three times. Then the spirit guide said, "The Great Spirit is pleased and will grant your prayers."

But first they must wrestle again until the spirit guide is dead. "Remove my clothes," he said, "and leave my body on the ground." Sadly the young

shaman followed these commands, and went home. Later he came back. The body was gone. But the tips of the spirit wrestler's green headdress were rising up out of the earth. Soon it grew into a plant as tall as the shaman.

And that's how the Ojibway received the gift of corn.

— A Story from the Ojibway (with many variations)

Gardeners are comfortable with death. Perhaps working inside the cycle of seeding, to planting out, to lifting and heaping and decay is a comfort when we are in despair.

When a dear friend of ours died, many expressed their grief by collecting masses of autumn flowers, arranging them on every windowsill in the church that held his funeral.

Later, they planted a garden in his memory. When there is a complete absence of words to adequately express feeling, we turn to symbols. Flowers speak powerfully of resurrection. The story told throughout North and South America of the dying and rising corn warrior (in some places it is about Mother Maize who dies to feed her children) is about this fusion. So is a story retold, below, from the gospel of John.

One morning, after Jesus had been killed, his friend Mary went to the tomb. When she looked inside —

because the entrance stone had been removed –
she saw two angels dressed in white. They asked her
why she was weeping and she said, "They have taken
away my Lord, and I do not know where they have
laid him." After Mary had said this, she turned around
and saw Jesus standing there. But she did not know it
was Jesus.

He said to her, "Woman, why are you weeping?
Whom are you looking for?" Supposing him to be the
gardener, Mary said to him, "Sir, if you have carried
him away, tell me where you have laid him and I will
take him away."

Jesus said to her, "Mary!"

And she said "Rabbouni!" (which means Teacher).

I have always loved this odd narrative. According to the group of
biblical scholars called the Jesus Seminar, not a word of it really
happened. I don't care, of course. Whether or not it is history is
completely beside the point. Like the Ojibway story of the gift of
corn, this is a myth so rich in meaning that it informs my life.

The part I love most is that Jesus is mistaken for a gardener.

That's not because I want to cast all gardeners in some
holy light, although that's tempting. It's because the image is
so delightful: Jesus sweaty and physical and real, not clothed
in white – gardeners don't wear white for long – but dressed
humbly and looking competent.

I love it, too, because of Mary's notion that this gardener might have carried away Jesus' body and placed it somewhere else. "Tell me where you have laid him and I will take him away," she says.

The implication is not that the gardener buried it, or hid it, or threw it on a trash heap, but that he had laid him down, gently, carefully, with respect. And now Mary offers to take on this generous task, the respectful care of the dead. When she does, she sees her friend alive. Out of his death something powerful and life-giving was given, just as the green tips of the spirit guide's headdress signaled the coming of the precious corn.

GIFTS OF LIFE FROM DEATH

We need such generous gifts today. One by one the voices of the earth are falling silent. Massive forests once cleaned the air, breathing for the earth; now floods and landslides, erosion and global warming show how deeply humans have wounded the lungs of the planet.

We've been doing this for a very long time. As historical philosopher Ronald Wright points out in *A Short History of Progress*, "the Athenians became alarmed by deforestation early in the sixth century BCE. Greek city populations were growing quickly at the time, most of the timber was already cut, and the poor were farming goat-stripped hills with disastrous results."

The Autumn Sonnets: Sonnet 2

If I can let you go as trees let go
Their leaves, so casually, one by one
If I can come to know what they do know,
That fall is the release, the consummation,
Then fear of time and the uncertain fruit
Would not distemper the great lucid skies
This strangest autumn, mellow and acute.
If I can take the dark with open eyes
And call it seasonal, not harsh or strange
(For love itself may need a time to sleep),
And, treelike, stand unmoved before the change,
Lose what I lose to keep what I can keep,
The strong root still alive under the snow,
Love will endure – if I can let you go.

— May Sarton

Gardening is one of the slowest of arts, asking patience and foresight and some simple manual labour in exchange for its ephemeral beauties. What the gardener plants in spring is not so much seeds and seedlings as hope.

– Jennifer Bennett and
Turgid Forsyth,
The Harrowsmith Annual Garden

The Greeks tried desperately to stop the damage. They struggled with rural poverty, tried to change damaging farming practices, and even offered grants to those who would plant olive trees. That would have slowed the erosion, but, says Wright, "funding and political will were unequal to the task."

Perhaps it still is. And this time, deforestation is global, not regional. It is very hard not to despair, especially when humans show such remarkable and erroneous adaptability to changed circumstances. A recent interview with a tourism promoter in my northern region featured the expert remarking cheerfully that with global warming's effect on precipitation patterns we must expect much less snow. Snowmobiling as a tourist attraction will suffer. Other sports will have to take their place.

There seemed no concern for the health of forests, rivers, farmland, and gardens. How are we to grow food without water? Eventually, social pressures will become unbearable, as larger populations try to survive on smaller chunks of arable land – just like the Greeks, and the Sumerians before them, and many civilizations to follow.

And yet Jesus the gardener, at the moment of Mary's deepest despair, calls her name. Mary. And she turns and says to him in Hebrew, "Rabbouni! Teacher!" Indeed. Gardeners teach us about hope.

HOW TO HOPE

One of Canada's most loved theologians, Douglas John Hall, in a book called *Hope for the World*, describes the "covert despair" with which we are afflicted in affluent countries. It is a despair we do not even admit to ourselves. He links it to the organized decimation of the natural world that progresses all around us.

But each spring, in my garden, I rake leaves away from the front beds near the road, piled there to protect them from road salt. I rake and pray for drenching rains to wash the toxic crystals away. Of course, there is no "away." There is only the lake.

And then I watch the plants. By some miracle, most survive, although the ones at the far corner, where the biggest piles of snow are blown up by the plow, are stunted. One year I lost a lovely peony. Its leaves were few and misshapen. Finally, I dug it up to throw on the compost heap.

Except I couldn't quite do it. Some children, welcoming me as a guest in their church, had given it to me. So I planted it at the back of a nursery bed and forgot it. The next spring it appeared fresh and new, undamaged.

Against all reason, this gives me hope. I can't help it. I know that the earth cannot bounce back forever. I know that, as Hall says, "sooner or later (sooner, if most ecologists are right), the possessing peoples, too, will be brought up short against the limitations of earth's bounty and the seeming resilience of the natural order. Then, however, it may be too late."

I know this, but I hope anyway.

the best revenge is
writing poetry
is gardening forever
covering ancient and
bitter brick with
geranium sweetheart roses
and virginal calla lilies

wondering how
these things can mean
so much more to me
year after year,
than I can, without them.

– LAURIE KRUK, FROM "IN WINDSOR, ONTARIO, ON BABA'S 85TH BIRTHDAY"

New Meaning

Hall himself is one source of hope. He suggests that we need a new framework of meaning, that the old one has not survived the assault of modernity. Science, computers – perhaps our own great power to damage the earth that gives us life – have made it hard to hold the old stories in our hearts. The Green Man, the Celts' beloved personification of spring, is no longer a fixture in our planting times.

But how do we create new meaning? The narratives that shape our thinking come unexpected, when we are looking for something else. Meaning is, in this respect, like happiness or a poem. We can only rejoice when it appears.

And yet gardeners say things without words. Perhaps we have a structure of meaning that might work – meaning expressed by beauty in the face of the world's despair; in the nicotiana that grows six feet tall and that floods the neighborhood with the scent of flowering tobacco, the sacred smoke of the gods.

Meaning is a structure built of myth and mystery and ancient wisdom. In our gardens, we touch that mystery as we set about the tasks of our earliest ancestors: digging, planting seed, gathering fruit. Few occupations today are as simply reminiscent of the past.

I feel close to those forebears when I plant my clay pots, for instance, simple and fragile, not so different from the earliest vessels humans made. And when I watch the way certain plants at certain seasons leap thirstily at life, I find I believe – as they did – that the earth is alive and ensouled. I believe that what some call Gaia loves us, and I love her back.

Stories people have long told come to life in the garden. The green feathered headdress of the spirit wrestler; the elm and ash who were the first Norse people; the gardener who is the holy one, Jesus; these stories can help us offer healing to the living earth.

A GARDENER'S RELIGION

If we are to have these stories, though, we must honor the spirituality that was here before many of us came to this land. We need to learn how to gratefully love creation, as indigenous people do and as we have forgotten how to do. We need to heal the ache we feel when the world is not as it should be, when forests are clear-cut and lovely old buildings are torn down and the water is not good to drink.

The great literary critic Northrop Frye said such healing is the job of the educated imagination. That imagination reveals "the real world, the real form of human society hidden behind the one we see."

When I sing a Celtic hymn attributed to St. Patrick, with its deep faith in the physical strength of earth and heavens, perhaps I am already honoring that vision of a whole and healed Creation.

The tree which moves some to tears of joy is in the eyes of others only a green thing that stands in the way. Some see nature all ridicule and deformity… and some scarce see nature at all. But to the eyes of the man [sic] of imagination, nature is imagination itself.
– WILLIAM BLAKE

It goes in part like this:
     I bind unto myself today
     the virtues of the starlit heaven,
     the glorious sun's life-giving ray,
     the whiteness of the moon at even,
     the flashing of the lightning free,
     the whirling wind's tempestuous shocks,
     the stable earth,
     the deep salt sea,
     around the old eternal rocks.

In fact, the spirituality I wish for is found in this story, which comes from my own life.

A friend of mine, who is Ojibway, brought me a big clump of sweet grass for my garden. "This is the hair of Mother Earth," she said, and I accepted with gratitude, because those who know where sweet grass is to be found don't usually tell, and it is an act of some significance to dig it up. So I planted it, and the sweet grass rejoiced greatly in the rich soil of that already full garden bed.

"The hair of Mother Earth has taken over my garden," I informed my friend, and she laughed immoderately.

"Did I forget to tell you to keep it contained?" she said.

So I pulled it up and put it in a huge bucket. But I didn't get all the roots. Some of it stayed in the garden and settled happily around an ancient peony I inherited from my Scottish grandfather, a peony I have moved with me from house to house, wherever we have gone. And in the right season, when the peony blooms, and it rains, if you stand in that corner of the garden you can smell the sweet grass and the peony mingled together.

And that is the scent of paradise and home.

This would be a new structure of meaning, new life forged out of two ancient spiritualities – 2000 years of Christianity, and millennia of indigenous, earth-centered spirituality.

It is summed up in a photo I saw once on a newspaper front page. The story was about a massive protest against logging at Clayoquot Sound and the picture was a close-up of a young woman sitting in the middle of the road to halt the logging trucks. Her hair was wreathed in leaves and her eyes, serene, seemed fixed on the imaginative vision Northrop Frye described: "the real world, the real form of human society hidden behind the one we see." The world where the living forests are honored.

New life out of ravaged trees; hope out of despair for the Mother Earth. Gardeners and all who love the land know that out of death can always spring new life.

....if I wanted to have a happy garden, I must ally myself with my soil; study and help it to the utmost, untiringly. Always, the soil must come first.
– MARION CRAN,
IF I WERE BEGINNING AGAIN

6

Gardening as Spiritual Practice

And for all this, nature is never spent;
· There lives the dearest freshness deep down things;
And though the last lights off the black West went
Oh, morning, at the brown brink eastward,
springs –
Because the Holy Ghost over the bent
World broods with warm breast and ah!
bright wings
– GERARD MANLEY HOPKINS

W e garden for our soul's sake. If it was just about burning calories, we could walk for an hour each day and save all the money we spend on shovels, new plants, and manure.

The many great gardens of the world, of literature and poetry, of painting and music, of religion and architecture, all make the point as clear as possible: The soul cannot thrive in the absence of a garden. If you don't want paradise, you are not human; and if you are not human, you don't have a soul.

— Thomas Moore,
The Re-Enchantment of Everyday Life

But competence in nourishing the soul is like any other skill. It involves practice, which my dictionary defines as "the repeated performance of an activity in order to perfect a skill."

Such discipline – at the violin, at medicine, at law, at spirituality – requires time. In my life, especially in winter, there is never enough time. My soul begins to jabber; the prevailing metaphor for my life is a rat on a treadmill, running, running. I do not actually run marathons; my treadmill is a desk and it wrecks the body for physical speed.

But in the midst of this comes March, planting season. Exhausted already, I nonetheless do what I have always done. Dig my way into the shed (still banked with snow) where the planting trays are stored, cart them into the house and wash them one by one in the laundry tubs, for they must be clean to fend off microbes that would destroy the germinating seeds.

I fill them one by one with growers' mix, and water, and plant, dusting tiny seeds over the soil and placing the finished trays, hopefully, on an old electric blanket under a weird contraption of grow lights I have rigged up in the basement.

I do this over and over and nothing happens. I begin to snap at people, pressed as I am by the stuff of life: crises, deadlines, celebrations, dinners to cook, and interesting scandals in the news.

But I keep planting, tenderly, because I have saved or bought these precious seeds, and this is what I have always done, and my father before me.

And one morning, when – water sprayer in hand – I check the trays for drought, ah! Two tiny green leaves. I remove my glasses and bend my nose almost to the soil. Two more over here.

I am filled with light. It was thus, I believe, with my ancestors 10,000 years ago. No grow lights, no sprayers, no clever colored packages of seeds; but the same annual bending to the soil, the discovery of new leaves, the same expansion of the spirit.

This is gardening as spiritual practice. It is kin to what some do in church, synagogue, mosque, temple, or around a sacred fire: praying, singing, kneeling, chanting. It is holy ritual, the repeated effort to draw closer to the Creator whose joy and beauty suffuses the earth. "The world is charged with the glory of God," says poet Gerard Manley Hopkins. "It will flame out like shining from shook foil."

So spring after spring, year after year, I watch the tiny seeds grow and I am dazzled by the flame. I have no doubt at all that to draw closer to the land is to draw closer to God.

BODY PRAYER

Most of us do spiritual practice in the garden unaware, or not naming it even to ourselves. Prayer, for example, is universal in every faith. There have been too many earnest plaques sold in too many gift shops to put the words "prayer" and "garden" into one sentence without wincing. But the garden is where I practice body prayer, silently bending to tuck in a new seedling; stretching to prune, to deadhead; or kneeling to pry out a stubborn weed.

This prayer has no words, not even those unspoken. I yearn for the small seedling to do well. I wince for the cut of the pruner on the tree, and hope for it to heal. With these intentions toward wholeness, I serve the earth and the notion of beauty that I carry in my mind – the idea that blossom and leaf and scent and texture will someday combine to make my heart pause with pleasure.

This is a servanthood that engages my whole being. A long time ago, I embarked on a pilgrimage with a group of nuns from the United States. We were on our way to Honduras, where the American government was building a field hospital in preparation for invading Nicaragua; or at least persuading their surrogates to do so. They needed, these nuns explained, to get on a plane and go there. To place their bodies in the place of evil, to try to stop it. Their journey and their physical presence was a spiritual act.

*Some keep the Sabbath
going to Church,
I keep it
staying at Home –
With a Bobolink
for a Chorister,
And an Orchard,
for a Dome.*

— EMILY DICKINSON

119

I think about those women often, about their single-minded understanding that prayer may require the body, as well as the heart and soul and mind. It is necessary at times to put your entire physical being, every muscle, every cell, into one powerful yearning plea to God.

And so I put my winter-soft, desk-weary body into the task of serving beauty, bending and stooping, lifting and digging, raking away the wet leaves that cover the beds.

Then April comes and the snow retreats to dirty remnants in the corners of the yard, and I unwrap the heavy clay pots from the multiple tarps that protect them from freezing water, which would crack them.

One by one, I haul them to their summer home on the driveway. Then, slowly, I fill them, first with leaves scraped off the beds, and then rich compost. I am struck, as I note this year's new chips and cracks, by their fragility. These are simple earthen vessels, once-fired, unglazed, not hardened for frost. They are made in the south and if they were openly exposed to a northern winter they would simply crumble and turn back into earth.

But although they have come from far away, I believe they belong here in my garden. They remind me of the fragility and permanence of Mother Earth herself. As humans, we transform the clay and shape it as we will. But ultimately, despite my best efforts, these pots will return to dust. And so will I, my bones

Without the body, the wisdom of the larger self cannot be known.
— JOHN CONGER

and tissue melting back into the earth from which I came. The earth will always have her due.

I rejoice in this.

So does author and theologian Rosemary Ruether, who meditates on this process in *Gaia and God*.

Our bodies disintegrate into organic matter, to enter the cycle of decomposition and recomposition as other entities… The material substances of our bodies live on in plants and animals, just as our own bodies are composed from minute to minute of substances that were once parts of other animals and plants, stretching back through time to prehistoric ferns and reptiles, to ancient biota that floated in the primal seas of earth.

There is nothing pleasanter than spading when the ground is soft and damp.
— John Steinbeck

Thus we are connected to one another, each fragile, weighty pot and me. And surely my pleasure in their shape and form, and in my own strength to lift and fill them, and in my work to help them flood with color – surely that self-consciousness is reflected in what some call God, and some call Gaia, and what Hopkins calls the Holy Ghost who "over the bent /World broods with warm breast and ah! bright wings."

Ruether goes on. "Our kinship with all earth creatures is global, linking us to the whole living Gaia today," she says. "It also spans the ages, linking our material substance with all the beings that have gone before us on the earth and even to the dust of exploding stars."

So the little piece of stardust that I once was sprinkles tough early seeds on the soil in my once-stardust pots: alyssum, California poppy, calendula. And soon – because this is practice, "the repeated performance of an activity in order to perfect a skill" – soon my spirit strengthens.

God must be pleased. I and God rejoice in the strength I thought I might have lost, and in the pots that earnestly line the driveway, ready to burst into purple and silky gold. They are proof of my obedience to the beauty that is God's face, proof of my homage to the great holy greening force that continually makes and remakes the world.

Thanksgiving Prayer

One October, oh, years ago, in the little, mostly rural congregation where we lived, the congregation gave up the traditional harvest theme for Thanksgiving Sunday. In a desire to honor those who worked in a nearby factory as well as those who worked on farms, we decorated the front of the church with the wide range of translucent plastic containers manufactured at the factory. That action had a point. We were trying to say that we were grateful to God for all good things, including the oil that produced this plastic and underpinned this steady source of employment.

But we missed something: the terrible irony of using up this precious oil in the very act of thanking God for doing so. The pumpkins and squash, carrots and potatoes that had graced our sanctuary for many years would grow again, year after year, as long as gardens existed in which to plant them.

But the petroleum spun into these vessels and burned in our cars would not. If our generation, or the next generation, uses up these ancient forests pressed into black oil by the weight of countless millennia, they cannot be replaced. And our great-great-grandchildren will doubtless wonder how we could have turned something so priceless into plastic bins for tea and sugar, or plastic bags to throw away.

In *The Wisdom of the Elders*, scientist David Suzuki tells the story of a Maya Indian in the Guatemalan highland who pauses to pray gratefully to Pokohil, the forest guardian, after he has killed two deer.

O Pokohil, today you have shown favour,
And have given some of your beasts,
some of your deer,
Thank you Pokohil.
See, I bring you flowers for your deer.
Perhaps you have counted them.
Two of them are missing…

Like the Mayan, I believe God notes the way we use the world, notes that the vast reserves of oil are growing thin. Perhaps God counts the barrels extracted from beneath the deserts and the oceans, and knows how much oil is left.

We didn't heap the altar again with plastic. But 30 years after that Thanksgiving Sunday, my cupboard still boasts the plastic containers from that day. I use them. I try very hard to be very grateful for them. Because they were warmly and lovingly given to me that Sunday, and I know they cost the earth.

Connection with gardens, even small ones, even potted plants, can become windows to the inner life. The simple act of stopping and looking at the beauty around us can be prayer.
– Patricia R. Barrett,
The Sacred Garden

STILLNESS AND GENEROSITY

Such prayers of gratitude for what is taken are practiced easily in the garden. Stillness helps. Pausing to look carefully is a crucial spiritual practice. In June, for instance (when gardeners lean away lest exuberant growth knock us off our feet) the throat aches to know that tomorrow will not be just this way. Today's peculiar brew of leaf and sun and buzzing insect will not be seen or heard again. Standing still, inhaling, and listening are rituals of gratitude.

Such rituals require no discipline. With no effort at all on my part, the garden lifts me off my treadmill, seducing me in the morning into quietly having one more cup of coffee, while I gaze at it; and at evening into just one more peaceful walk around it in the fading light.

Prayers of gratitude are expressed in giving, too. That's easy, given God's extravagance. Gardeners love to appear at someone's door, holding out freshly divided perennials that are looking for a home. I poll the neighborhood carefully, watching for victims.

"I'm not a gardener," they sometimes say.

"Not yet," I reply sweetly to myself, hoping for an invitation to tour their backyard and offer advice.

It's not just orphaned perennials that arrive at the door. One early spring, a long time ago, a friend's barn burned. We all mourned and brought soup and homemade bread. Two weeks later, she was at my downtown home bearing an enormous bunch of fresh-picked asparagus.

"Don't you need that?" I burst out (impolitely) appalled at her giving away her produce in the face of recent tragedy.

She was rightly startled. "But I wanted you to have some of the first asparagus," she said, and smiled.

It was, of course, an act of gratitude: for friends, for love, for safety from the fire that claimed only boards and stones, not life. The cows were already in the field.

We feasted on this bounty and rejoiced.

PRAYERS WITH WORDS

To be true to the spiritual practice of my Celtic ancestors, I must sometimes pray in words as well. Prayer was something they did throughout the day, constantly underlining each act in a world where they felt surrounded by angels and visitors from heaven.

I try to do that too. Early one summer morning not long ago, I was watering my still not-drought-proofed rock garden with a hose. I heard a noise beside me. It was a white-tailed deer, who had wandered up the railway line into the city's heart. Now she was in my backyard looking lost. She may have been thirsty and heard water, I don't know.

We stared at each other for a time, astonished. Then she leaped around the yard, seeking a way out. Finally, rejecting the street that runs along the front, she sailed over the compost pile and through the backyards of sleepy neighbors, all no doubt as startled as myself.

"I think," one of the children from next door confided to me later, "that deer thought your garden looked like a forest."

I have loved the child ever since.

And I have loved that deer, gracing me with her early morning presence. No doubt I would be less pleased if she returned often to nibble on the lilies. But my Celtic ancestors understood St. Patrick himself to be close to deer. "In Gaelic myth and story, the deer is not merely an animal," says author and theologian Herbert O'Driscoll in *The Leap of the Deer*. "In more than one story, Irish saints have taken upon themselves the shape of a deer, to avoid danger or flee from enemies. It is said thus Patrick and his monks reached Tara and the high king's palace as they went on Easter Eve to challenge the druids and the old pagan deities."

And so I regarded my deer, in the Celtic spirit, as a visitor from heaven. And in the Celtic spirit I have made a prayer,

which I say to myself from time to time:

    Blessings on all animals of the forest
        Our kin
    Blessings on all birds of the sky
        Our friends
    Blessings on the loveliness of plants
        Our joy
    And blessings on all visitors from heaven
        Our kin.

Spiritual Practice Together

All of this sounds as if I am suggesting that the garden can substitute for communal spiritual practice: "I'll just worship the Creator in the garden this morning." It is something I have whispered to myself from time to time. But while the garden has its own precious spiritual discipline – the moments of awe at the fresh green of spring, the ritual journeys to the blue box and the compost heap, the generous giving that is a form of gratitude, and thankful prayer – there are times when spirituality is practiced with others.

Oh, there were anchorites, like Julian of Norwich, who walled themselves up in prayer and contemplation, and hermits who lived alone in the desert. But some of us need companions with whom to sing and pray and discuss the meaning of life and death.

For those who do, I believe the secret is to bring these communities of faith a little closer to the garden. Collective spiritual practice should confess our love for and relationship with the land, and not just on harvest holidays. "We need new psalms and meditations," says Ruether, "to make this kinship vivid in our communal and personal devotions."

Poet Ray McGinnis, in *Writing the Sacred*, offers such a psalm.

I praise the maiden Africa,
who gave birth to earth to the beat of a drum,
who sent a crow across the universe to announce
its arrival,
who listened for a name, ancient as star or dirt,
to give to it,
who poured libations, breathed on it, tattooed and
shaped earth into oceans, continents.

I praise the mother India,
who washed the earth in the Ganges River,
who took it for an elephant ride,
who charmed earth with a snake, protected it with
a mongoose,
who rocked it to sleep.

I praise the old native crone,
who saw earth emerge from the sea on a turtle's back,
who blessed earth with sweet grass,
who wiped earth's brow,
who told earth stories of brother sun and sister moon.

But while McGinnis honors the earth in solitude here, sometimes such spiritual practice requires the presence of others. Some communities of faith plant vegetable gardens on their downtown city site, for instance, and use the produce for the food bank. Some plant flowers and simply offer the beauty to passersby. Some care for the environment and will turn out bearing pickets, to protect an escarpment or a lake.

Stan McKay, Cree elder and former national leader of my particular faith community, longs for "every congregation, in planning their worship, to allow at least four Sundays a year for worship outside," because we have "a limited perception of ways to be in relationship with God in the natural order."

Gardeners who live with the Creator every day – who see her in every new plant shouting its way out of the frozen earth – are ready to burst those limits. That is our gift to others and we can offer it in many ways.

People "need to take time to sit under trees," says Ruether, "look at water and the sky, observe small biotic communities of plants and animals with close attention, get back in touch with the living earth. We can start to release the stifled intuitive and creative powers of our organism, to draw and write poetry, and to know that we stand on holy ground."

We can plant our gardens boldly for those needing the touch of earth. My husband likes to invite people who are stressed into our quiet back garden, to walk and sit and

contemplate. I was fearful of this at first, worried that there might be so many visitors no one would be able to reflect in peace. But I have come to see this as an opportunity for warmth and greeting, not unease.

Because he's right.

This hospitality is the ultimate spiritual discipline and the hardest one for a solitary, introverted gardener to practice. To simply have an open heart. To welcome. To love those in need and to delight as they respond to beauty. To help form a community of friends who love the earth, what Ruether calls "strong base communities of celebration and resistance."

When it comes to the pain the earth endures, Ruether says, "being rooted in love for our real communities of life and for our common mother, Gaia, can teach us patient passion; passion that is not burnt out in a season but can be renewed, season after season. Our revolution is not just for us, but for our children, for the generations of living beings to come."

We cannot stop loving the earth because of oil slicks and massive clear-cuts, or too much asphalt or polluted seas. These desecrations make us want to turn our heads away. But contemplation of the garden gives us strength to resist earth's degradation. Prayerful confession of our part in this pain, tender rituals of planting, prayers for new growth, and graceful welcome to those who love the land: these are the spiritual practices of gardening.

7

Gardening as Resistance

Once upon a time, Persephone, the lovely daughter of the goddess Demeter, was abducted by Hades, lord of the Underworld. Demeter is the goddess of all green living things, honored on baking day as Grain-mother.

Without her daughter, Demeter went into mourning. The earth became brown and barren while she wandered and wailed for her child. Finally Jupiter, king of the gods, intervened. It was agreed that Persephone would rule as queen in the Underworld for three months each year. The rest of the time she would spend with her mother in the Upperworld, where all would flourish in the light of Demeter's joy.

— A Story from Ancient Greece

It is spring now. The days are getting longer. I have moved the seedlings upstairs from their basement warmth one flat at a time, to the sun porch off our bedroom. They rest on a long shelf rigged from an old pine board propped up by books, in front of the window. The small green plants have grown.

As the days grow warm, I carry them outside, to a sheltered place beside the tool shed with a fence on one side and the house on the other. I tie up a tarp, just for this season, to keep the hottest rays of the sun at bay. Seedlings sunburn as easily as children. I bring them inside, one tray after another, every night that feels like frost.

When the little plants are strong, sometime after the long weekend in May, planting begins, the hardiest plants first. I will be in the garden at dawn. Young Desmond, across the street, who rises early too – he's three – will shout "Hello!" from his upstairs bedroom window. We will wave at each other in mutual delight.

Stories of the garden will ring in my ears. The green-feathered spirit-guide, wrestled to death, for corn. The hand of Eve, reaching for the apple. Odin making men and women out of trees. I will look up into the tall spruce and see Tane-mahuta the forest-god, keeping the sky and earth apart, and Demeter happily making all things grow.

I am part of this and I rejoice.

By mid-June, I will be replete with seeds and recollected stories. The slugs will eat some seedlings and I will suspect earwigs in the death of others.

But every year a multitude of plants survive, shaking off their predators and reaching for the sun. The pots that line the driveway will bloom early – California poppies, Schizanthus, candytuft – coaxed by heat rising from the asphalt I despise. The newest neighbors on the block will confess how puzzled they were by all these pots of, they assumed, herbs and how could anyone need so many?

At the end of June I will stop to breathe.

I imagine all this now, at my desk in the lengthening evening, seed catalogues still piled high, but consulted less often than in February. I consider the revolution gardeners carry in their souls. And I recall another story.

Once King Ahasuerus, ruler of 127 provinces, gave a banquet lasting seven days, in the enclosed garden of his palace...The garden had hangings of white and blue linen, fastened with cords of white linen and purple material to silver rings on marble pillars. There were couches of gold and silver on a mosaic pavement of porphyry, marble, mother-of-pearl and other costly stones. Wine was served in goblets of gold, each one different from the other, and the royal wine was abundant.

Queen Vashti gave a banquet for the women of the palace at the same time.

On the seventh day, when King Ahasuerus was

A person who undertakes to grow a garden at home, by practices that will preserve rather than exploit the economy of the soil, has his mind precisely against what is wrong with us... What I am saying is that if we apply our minds directly and competently to the needs of the earth, then we will have begun to make fundamental and necessary changes in our minds. We will begin to understand and to mistrust and to change our wasteful economy, which markets not just the produce of the earth, but also the earth's ability to produce.

– Wendell Berry

merry with wine, he told the seven eunuchs who attended him to bring Queen Vashti to him with the royal crown on her head. He wanted all the men to gaze on her beauty, for she was a very beautiful woman. But when they conveyed the king's order to Queen Vashti, she refused to come.

This narrative from Hebrew scriptures offers – in addition to a remarkable courtyard – a highly subversive woman. Although the king's word was law, she refused to attend a drunken bash, at which (it seems) she would wear the royal crown and nothing else. The king wished to display her beauty. She said no.

It was a revolutionary moment.

Vashti is like Demeter pacing the barren earth, refusing to participate in spring. They resisted powers greater than their own.

This Vashti-like resistance is important to gardeners, because creating beauty for its own worthless sake, and enjoying vegetables without benefit of long-distance, energy-costly transportation is now about refusal. It is a revolutionary lack of submission to the cultural wisdom that declares that profit is more important than beauty and the planet's health.

The banquet of greed now underway is one that gardeners are pleased not to attend. We imagine a new kingdom, where all that is harmful to the earth is banished.

Here's a pointed creation story from Judaism's book of commentary, the Talmud.

In the beginning, on the third day, God made the plants, including the giant cedars of Lebanon. The same day God also created iron, for axes to cut the cedars down, if they should grow too tall and arrogant. On the sixth day, God sent the angel Gabriel to bring soil from the four corners of Earth, with which to make humans. But when Gabriel set out, he discovered that Earth didn't want to give up any soil to make humans. Earth knew these humans would someday ruin her, despite her beauty.

So God alone scooped up the soil and made the humans…

In the end, we will conserve only what we love; we will love only what we understand; and we will understand only what we have been taught.

— BABA DIOUM

I don't know why humans developed herbicides and other things that ruin earth. What provokes such terror of dandelions? I do know that all fear of life ends, eventually, in war. Not a war on small yellow flowers and creeping spiders, but on each other.

I think we must be watchful with our children. They must have gardens – even on a balcony – and learn that bugs, and even weeds, belong in them as surely as humans do. We cannot have them stamping on an earthworm, just because it is; any more than we can have drivers swerving to run over a porcupine, or a snake or a turtle, just because they can.

This is a job for parents in postmodern times, when most of us are generations removed from agricultural life. We have to find ways to keep the connection to the land alive, to prevent earth's beauty – as the Talmudic story warns – from being ruined. If our children forget that we are bound hip and thigh to the land, we are doomed.

There is no place in this garden
for a 707 or any
aluminum wing

only the first flight of leaves

tracers of bees, caterpillars, small
reddish moths

and the rain

no place for gods, the fission
or fusion of Zeus

Promethean fire
would make matchwood of the picket fence weathering grey

half a bird's egg is sufficient
proof of violence

sleek stepping stones, no flood

like earth
this remnant of an orchard's vulnerable
to heavenly waste

the airways leak

yet a body might grow quiet in this modest space

it's not the end of the war
but the raids are seasonal, include
some heavy robins, spring's

green flak

— D. G. Jones, "There Is No Place"

143

To forget how to dig
the earth and
to tend the soil is
to forget ourselves.
—Mahatma Gandhi

Remembered Resistance

In our gardens, we keep this vision of connection. It compels some out to plant public gardens and others to save the forests, and some of us to simply make loveliness at home. Even there, we are a force, armed with hoes and straw hats and little flats of seedlings. Eden exists within us. Sometimes it drifts away, our vision, like Avalon in the mist. But the memory persists and we struggle on trying to re-create the peaceable kingdom.

Such a world, dreamed by gardeners, might look like this…

We would use less asphalt for driveways and parking lots. It bubbles hot in the summer, destroys the life of the soil beneath, and lets rainwater run away uselessly into the storm sewers.

We would insist that all businesses seeking to build industrial parks, chain restaurants, big box stores, and new commercial buildings agree to plant a specific number of shade trees before receiving a building permit. Parking lots especially should be well-supplied with trees, which would lessen the blast of air conditioning required to make a vehicle habitable after a few stationary hours on a hot day.

Large buildings would save on energy for cooling if they grew vines up their walls. That would require earth next to their foundations, which could host flowers as well as vines. Many structures sit on their parking lots, concrete butting securely against concrete, as if a stray dandelion might bring down the entire structure.

Gardening should be going with nature, not against it. Once you have healthy plants and cleaned-up soil, not only will your plants be stronger and more able to withstand any onslaught of disease and munching on by unwanted pests, but you'll feel better… I haven't found it harder or more time-consuming to garden ecologically. When we learn to respect nature and follow nature's laws we will make gorgeous gardens.

— Marjorie Harris,
Favorite Garden Tips

145

We would plant flowers everywhere: boxes on apartment balconies, in front of stores, hanging from lamps, and oh yes, vines climbing every lamp post.

We would use less salt on winter roads and on parking lots. What if everyone knew how the ancient Sumerians, having discovered the joys of irrigation (but not knowing that water leaches salt out of arid soils), were slowly stricken into famine by salinization? We would put snow tires on our cars to keep from skidding and cut back sharply on the salt we spray to melt the ice.

Traffic would be slowed, if there were trees and boulevards on residential streets. Municipalities could buy large quantities of tree seedlings, and homeowners and renters alike could plant them on Earth Day for the common good.

In my own city, willing volunteers created a communal garden in the middle of the downtown, where an old store had burned. It provides vegetables and companionship and makes our damaged city center whole and healthy.

Hundreds of volunteers work on the city waterfront, rejuvenating and improving municipal beds. Schools plant trees and flowers. I admire this greatly and dream of more: vines on every chain-link fence, city entrances alight with wildflowers, so many big old trees that every group of children could have a tree house, parks where old people could sit in the shade on summer afternoons and watch them play.

The thing is, gardeners are in love with a beauty inherent in the earth. We just try to help people see it. The whole earth is a garden that we have been given by our Creator. Our own vegetable patches and perennial borders, boxes of plants that grace apartment balconies, vivid borders installed by civic-minded mall owners, old downtowns exploding with tough petunias in huge baskets from every lamppost – all these teach us that life is not solely about achievement. It is about beauty for its own profitless, extravagant sake. It is about stubborn resistance to all who would harm the earth. It is about living in obedience to sun and rain and living in gratitude for this lovely, sacred, vital planet.

*Today there are many signs
that our culture is starting
to reconsider its drive
to colonize and exploit
the rest of the planet.
The search for spiritual
reconciliation is taking
many different forms:
finding virtue in crystals,
looking for guidance
from the movement of
the planets, submitting
to the demands of sects and cults, seeing rebirth in new
forms of old religions, making pilgrimages, gathering at
sacred sites. All these and many other expeditions into the
"supernatural" or "paranormal" represent a widespread,
deeply felt longing for wholeness and purpose on this
earth. Theologians and ecologists are finding common
ground as they explore the need to recognize the sacred in
the here-and-now, rather than in the hereafter, and try to
help human beings return home to their place in creation.*

— David Suzuki, *The Sacred Balance*

Conclusion

*The foolish [person]
seeks happiness
in the distance,
the wise grows it
under his feet.*

– JAMES OPPENHEIM

KEEPING THE CONNECTION

Spirituality is about connection with God. Spiritual, says my dictionary, means "of, concerned with, or affecting the soul." Hence these stories of gods and goddesses, Demeter and Mother Maize, Papatuanuku and Gaia.

But I began this book with the story of a little girl in a rowboat, a four-year-old, who understood that she was one with all that surrounded her: her father at the oars, the water in which she trailed her hand, the white pine and birch that crowded the shoreline, the approaching dock, the hot sun.

*Heaven is under
our feet as well as over
our heads.*

– THOREAU

I was that child and as I grew I tried very hard to destroy that mystical connection with creation. It hurt too much. As the years passed, it became unsafe to drink water straight from the lake, as we had always done. Many trees were cut down, necessarily, I was assured. My father got a better job and we moved away. The rowboat is rotted and gone.

My father died.

But that long-ago child still understands certain stories from around the world, because she felt that connection one time. As I write these closing sentences, for instance, all over the world people similarly anchored to their land are being harshly forced from it. In the Mexican province of Chiapas, 5000 small subsistence farmers are being forced off their land each month. The North American Free Trade Agreement has allowed their country to be flooded with cheap, subsidized imports, including genetically modified corn. The small indigenous farmers cannot compete, even though they are the people of the corn. Even though Mexico is where maize originated, and where thousands of varieties are carefully preserved in the ancient way, seeds saved and passed from one generation to another.

I understand this careful preservation. Gardeners understand that these seeds and the land that nourishes them are sacred.

Nobel Peace Prize winner Rigoberta Menchu – driven off her traditional land in Guatemala in particularly bloody

clearances – describes the rituals that surrounded the annual planting of the corn in her Mayan village. They requested the earth's permission to cultivate her, and in every house they burned candles. "Then we bring out the seeds we will be sowing…before the seeds are sown in the earth, we perform a ceremony. We choose two or three of the biggest seeds and place them in a ring, candles representing the earth, water, animals, and the universe… The seed is honored because it will be placed in something sacred – the earth – and because it will multiply and bear fruit the next year. We do it mainly because the seed is something pure, something sacred."

It is my role as a gardener to remember the sacredness of the earth. Doing so means picking up the connection with it that the four-year-old painfully put down all those years ago. It means rediscovering ties with our cousins on the land, such as the farmers of Chiapas and Guatemala, who become migrant workers, picking our fruit for low wages and few benefits, far from their home. Or they make the dangerous illegal border crossings that allow them to send money home to feed their families, since their corn can no longer do that.

We gardeners do what we can. We march or pray, and teach our children how it is with farmers around the world. We try – like the wonderful volunteers in my hometown who tend our waterfront and who plant gardens downtown – to honor the beauty of our earth so that people understand how precious it is.

This work keeps meaning in the old stories: Eve biting bravely into the apple of knowledge; Demeter raving for her daughter, withholding summer until she is safe; the druids studying in their sacred groves; the green warrior dying to give us corn.

And with our labor, we make a healing place – for ourselves and for the spirits who would join us in our gardens, and for others who need rest.

Most of all, we gather strength in our gardens. Whenever we pick up our hoe – not so different really from the hoe of a gardener in Kenya or Honduras – whenever we place a small green seedling in the ground, whenever we burrow a small hole with an old pencil and drop in a seed, or dig a larger one and plant a tree, we are making more durable the invisible web that connects all who love the land.

In all the ways each of us, one by one, cherishes creation, we add to her resilience.

And in so doing we pick up and hold close those small children we once were, the ones who followed their parents around the garden, who dug holes and planted leftover perennials and were delighted when they grew. They thought they were part of the land, those children who were us, at one with it, and whole.

And we will tell them they were right.

It is only when we are aware of the earth and of the earth as poetry that we truly live.
– HENRY BESTON, 1935, *HERBS AND THE EARTH*

153

Before the Common Era or Christian-Roman Era

35,000
Evidence from archeological sites indicates that Homo sapiens at the end of the Paleolithic period had knowledge of many plants derived from food gathering techniques. Different kinds of fruits, nuts, and roots were only gathered, not cultivated.

15,000
"A close acquaintance with cultivated plants and with the multitude of types and their differentiation into geographical groups as well as their frequently sharp physiological isolation from each other compel us to refer the very origin of cultivated plants to such remote epochs…" – N. I. Vavilov, *Origin and Geography of Cultivated Plants*, 1987.

8500
In Mesopotamia, humans raised domesticated goats, sheep, and real grains. Neolithic cultures involved farming.

8000
"Certain cereals and pulses (legumes) were domesticated in very ancient times. In about 8000 BC the Fertile Crescent of the Near and Middle East (present-day Syria, Iran, Iraq, Jordan, and Israel), wheats barley, lentil, pea, bitter vetch, chick-pea, and possibly faba bean, were brought into cultivation by the Neolithic people." – *The New Oxford Book of Food Plants*

7000
People in central America cultivate corn and other crops.
Rice cultivation in Yangtze Valley of China.
Apples cultivated in southwestern Asia.

6000
Evidence of cultivation of wheat (but not breadwheat), barley (naked, not hulled), and lentils were found in the Neolithic Greek cultures of Thessaly, Crete, and the Cyclades. Oranges cultivated in India and Tigris River Valley.
Cultivation of maize in Peru.

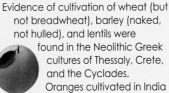

5000
Wild pod corn cultivated in the Tehuacan valley in Mexico. [Baker, 1978]
Millet grown along the Yellow River (Huang Ho) in China.
The Native people of North America inhabit river flood plains and cultivate crops.
Irrigation begins in the Middle East. [Heiser, 1990]
Cotton grown in Mexico.
Wine making in Iran.

4800
Archeological evidence from Tehuacan in south central Mexico shows that maize, squash, chili peppers, avocados, and amaranth were cultivated. [Heiser, 1990]

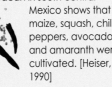

4500
Evidence of managed woodlands in Britain.

4000
Farming in Mesopotamia by Sumerians, Hittites.
Indus Valley agriculture is very extensive: wheat, peas, sesame seed, barley, dates, mangoes.

3900
Rice grown in Southeast Asia, Korat area of Thailand.

3500
Egyptian agriculture using extensive irrigation techniques. Egyptian garden art.

3000
Written manuals for the use of herbs in medicine exist in Mesopotamia (now Iraq) and in China.

Potatoes are cultivated in the Andes mountains of Peru.
Egyptians in the Nile Valley manufacturing and wearing cotton clothes.
Egyptian tomb paintings show walled gardens with fish ponds and fruit trees.
Olives cultivated in Crete and Syria.
Farming in India.

2700
Rhubarb cultivated in China for medicinal purposes.
Egyptians used over 500 plants, wild and cultivated, for medicinal purposes. Egyptian wine making.
Chinese Emperor Shen Nung's plant classification lists. Hemp cultivation in China.

2500
Farming in England.

2000
Native Americans are growing ma... varieties of corn, beans, squash, sunflowers, as well as using many wild plants as foc... Watermelon cultivated... Africa, tea and banan... in India, apples in the Indus Valley.

1750
The Hammurabic Code. Includes sections on maintaining irrigation canals and ditches, and property laws regarding gardens. Sumerian "Farmer's Almanac."

1495
One of the oldest surviving garden... plans is for the garden of a cou... official in Thebes.

1300
Ramses II has apples cultivated al... the Nile.

1275
The Torah establishes rules for kosher food.

1000
Irrigation begins in Mexico. [Heiser, 1990]

800
Farming in Africa.

This is an edited version of a much more extensive timeline created by Michael Garofalo. To view the original, full timeline please visit www.gardendigest.com.

)
ging Gardens of Babylon.
ar cane grown along the Indus
iver.

7
pocrates (circa 460–377) Greek
physician. Wrote 87 treatises.
Many herbal remedies.

2
totle (384–322) Greek philosopher
and scientist. Wrote 26 treatises on
natural science.
hange of information, seeds,
and plants between Greece and
Persia.

1
ory of Plants and Theoretical
Botany by Theophrastus.

1
curus (341–271) used a large
garden for gatherings and walks.

7
opulent and extensive gardens
and palace of the first Chinese
emperor Ch'in Shih Huang-ti
vere burned by peasants and
Confucian rebels.

)
rdens at Pompeii, Italy [Helphand,
977]
tivation and trade of coconuts
between East Africa and India.
Hopewellian farming culture in
Ohio, North America, is thriving.

)
nlin Yuan ("yuan" is Chinese for
"garden") occupied over 1000
m² and contained more than 300
palaces.

Roman's staple grain was spelt.
naturalist.

Common Era or Christian Era

250
The administrators of the Roman Empire (circa 100–500 CE) actively exchanged information on agriculture, horticulture, animal husbandry, hydraulics, and botany.
Seeds and plants were widely shared.

460
Chinese "scholar gardens."
Eggplants cultivated in China and India.

550
Domestication of coffee takes place in Arabia until 800. [Baker, 1978] (In the year 2000, coffee imports and exports are second only to oil on the world trade market.)

560
Ono No Imoko, Japanese Buddhist priest and scholar, living by a lake "ikebono," developed an elemental Ikebana flower arrangement style.

670
St. Fiacre – patron saint of gardeners (620–670)

750
Use of the Green Man in art and lore becomes widespread in Christian Europe.

760
Hindu and Arabic mathematicians and thinkers are using a decimal arithmetic.
Farmers and gardeners frequently keep detailed logs of their work, and decimal arithmetic is widely used to track important details, e.g., costs of plants and materials, percentage of plants in a batch of cuttings that took, quarts of berries picked, current supermarket price of fresh green beans, etc.

900
Tofu commonly eaten in China.

1085
The great Arab libraries in Toledo, Spain, provide Europeans access to sophisticated Islamic and Greek writings in science and agriculture.

1120
Manor system in Europe. A manor was roughly 900 to 2,000 acres of arable land.

1150
The use of windmills for grinding grains.

1191
Tea from China becomes popular in Japan.

1227
Vatican botanical garden founded. A medicinal or physic garden which still exists today, although in a different location.
St. Francis of Assisi (1182–1126). A holy man now known for his love of animals and nature, and his kindness.

1250
The Japanese Buddhist priest Eisai (1141–1215) utilized a tea ritual as practiced in Chinese Buddhist temples.
The wheelbarrow makes its way into European books.

1350
County gardens provide a retreat for those fleeing the plague.

1450
Emperor Yoshimasa of Japan made flower arrangement part of universal education.

1470
Ottoman Turks introduce coffee to Constantinople. "The world's first coffee shop, Kiva Han, opens in 1475."

1492
Voyage of Christopher Columbus from Spain to the edge of the Americas. The beginning of plant exchanges between Europe and the Americas.

1516
First use of the term "herbal" per the *Oxford English Dictionary*.

1533
Oldest university chair of botany in Europe, founded in Padua by the Venetian Republic.
Spaniards start caco tree plantations in Venezuela and Trinidad.

1535
Nature Mysticism of Heinrich Cornelius Agrippa of Nettesheim (1487–1535) and Theophrastus Para Isus (1493–1541).

1543
Europe's first bontanic garden, established in Pisa by botany professor Luca Ghini.

1550
The first printed almanacs in English become available.

1555
Carolus Clusius, Dutch botanist, cultivating tulip bulbs imported from Constantinople.

1570
Francisco Hernandez, private physician to Philip II of Spain, explores the New World and reports over 1,000 plants considered of medicinal value. This research was not published until 1651 as *Rerum Medicarum Novae Hispaniae.*

1583
De Plantis Libri. Andrea Cesalpino. A very important book in the history of botany. Plants grouped by physical characteristics (morphology) rather than by medicinal properties.

1586
Sir Francis Drake brings sassafras and potatoes from America to England. [Rupp, 1990]
The Good Huswifes Handmaid for Cookerie in Her Kitchen published.

1595
Floriculture and plant collecting are very popular in England and the Low Countries.

1600
European forests are becoming depleted and shortages of wood affect various industries.

1612
The beginning of tobacco cultivation in Virginia. Europeans are introduced to drinking tea.

1615
The English Hus-Wife "Contayning the inward and outward vertues which ought to be in a compleat woman; As, her skill in Physicke, Cookery, Banqueting-stuffe, Distillation, Perfumes, Wooll, Hemp, Flax, Dayries, Brewing, Baking, and all other things belonging to an houshould." Gervase Markham

1618
The Country House-Wife's Garden. William Lawson. Includes knot garden designs.

1621
The first American Thanksgiving feast was celebrated in Plymouth Colony by the pilgrims and Massasoit Indians.

1630
The Dutch soon begin growing tulips as a major cash crop.

1638
Honeybees introduced into the American colonies.

1646
The use of greens and vegetables in salads.

1648
Agrarian revolution underway in Europe due to advantages of new crops like potatoes.

1652
Coffee being used in England.

1670
First Scottish botanic garden, in Edinburgh.

1686
American kitchen gardens from 1600–1800 were planted based on astrology, featured many herbs, used raised beds well dunged and dug in the autumn, and were fenced in to keep animals out.

1701
The first agricultural machine, the seed drill, was invented by Jethro Tull.

1715
The four-field crop rotation (turnips, wheat, barley, and clover) was popularized by Charles Townshend.

1727
Coffee plantations established in Brazil. [Baker, 1978]

1732
Philip Miller of the Chelsea Physic Garden sends the first cotton seeds to Georgia, USA.

1729
Guillaume Beaumont (1650–1729) created the famous topiary garden at Levens Hall, Cumbria.

1753
Roses from China begin arriving in Europe.

1767
Lazzaro Spallanzani (1765–1767) experiments with sterilization.

1784
Seeds sold in paper packets by Shakers in New England.

1795
Nicholas Appert, a Frenchman, developed techniques for preserving foods by canning.

1797
Charles Newbold, a blacksmith in Burlington, N.J., introduced the cast-iron moldboard plow.

1800
"In 1800, approximately 75% of the population [America] were directly engaged in agricultural production. By 1850, it was less than 60% and by 1900, less than 40% were engaged in agricultur production." *Modern Agricultur*

1801
John Chapman, Johnny Applesee begins planting apple trees in th Ohio Valley.

1810
In England, Peter Durand, invents tin can for preserving foods.

1823
In France, Louis Bernard Rabaut invented an expresso coffee machine.

1826
Apple orchards in Canada.

[18]0
[ ] lawn mower invented in England [b]y Edwin Beard Budding.

[18]3
[Je]wish kosher food in the USA.

[18]1
[ ] potato famine begins.

[18]0
[ ] growth of railroad systems [a]round the world from 1850–1890 [g]reatly expands the marketing [o]ptions for agriculture.

1859
The bedding system is very popular: geometrical flower beds with colorful annuals, e.g., 40,000 bedding plants were set out in [H]yde Park, London, in 1859.

[18]3
[Sca]le insects destroy 2.5 million acres [o]f French vines.

[18]8
[ ]urbia, a planned community [o]utside Chicago, designed by [F. L]. Olmsted.

[18]73
[DDT] invented by Othmar Zeidler. Its [i]nsecticidal properties were not [e]xploited until the 20th century.

1876
The Effects of Cross and Self Fertilization in the Vegetable Kingdom. Charles Darwin.

1889
Charter Gas Engine Company gasoline tractor is manufactured and sold with success.

1894
Iceberg lettuce introduced by W. Atlee Burpee & Co.
Japanese Tea Garden in Golden Gate Park, San Francisco, is developed for Exposition.

1901
A yellow rose, *Soleil d'Or*, begins a new phase in rose breeding.

1904
American Horticultural Society established.
Chestnut tree blight begins in the Eastern United States and eventually destroys American chestnut trees.

1910
One American farmer produces enough to sustain seven people.

1920
American Orchid Society founded.

1923
The Spirit of the Garden. Martha Brookes Hutcheson. Garden design book with outstanding photographs.

1924
Commercial production of soybeans begins in the United States. [Baker, 1978]

1932
James Markham obtains the first patent issued for a tree – a special peach tree.

1934
The great dust storms in Midwest states and Canadian provinces begin.

1938
Food, Drug and Cosmetic Act in the USA. Federal and state laws aimed at improving in the quality of food manufacturing, processing, distributing, and retailing.
The Secret Garden. Frances Hodgson Burnett.

1943
DDT introduced to the USA.
Famine in Bengal: over 3 million people die.

1948
Our Plundered Planet. Fairfield Osborn. An early expose of the effects of DDT on wildlife.

1953
Francis Crick and James Watson discover the structure of DNA. Arguably the most important biological discovery of the 20th century.

1962
Silent Spring. Rachel Carson. The negative effects of agricultural chemicals.

1968
Whole Earth Catalog. Howard Rheingold.

1970
The first Earth Day celebrations and marches are organized.

1972
DDT usage banned in the United States by the EPA.
Paul Berg, molecular biologist, develops techniques for transferring one strand of DNA to another.

1973
The California Certified Organic Gardeners is organized by 50 farmers.

1979
International Federation of Organic Agriculture Movements is founded.

1980
First U.S. patent issued for a genetically engineered bacterial organism.
The Readers Digest Complete Library of the Garden.

1982
Richard St. Barbe Baker dies (1889–1982). Billions of trees have been planted as a result of reforestation projects he encouraged, inspired, or led.

One American farmer produces enough to sustain 78 people.

1994
First transgenetic food approved for sale in the USA – the Flavr Savr tomato.

1997
Development of a genetically altered potato with a BT gene that kills some insects.

2000
Nearly 50% of the world's labor force is employed in agriculture.

Bibliography

Bierlein, J. F. *Parallel Myths*. New York: Ballantine Wellspring, 1994.

Brueggemann, Walter, ed. *Hope for the World: Mission in a Global Context*. Louisville: Westminster John Knox Press, 2001.

Chamber, Douglas. *Stony Ground: The Making of a Canadian Garden*. Toronto: Vintage Canada, 1997.

de Waal, Esther. *Every Earthly Blessing: Recovering the Celtic Tradition*. Harrisburg: Morehouse Publishing, 1992.

Frye, Northrop. *The Educated Imagination*. Toronto: CBC Publications, 1963.

Gill, Sam D., and Irene F. Sullivan. *Dictionary of Native American Mythology*. New York: Oxford University Press, 1994.

Harris, Marjorie. *Favorite Garden Tips*. Toronto: HarperCollins Canada Ltd., 2003.

Herriot, Trevor. *Jacob's Wound: A Search for the Spirit of Wildness*. Toronto: McClelland and Stewart, 2004.

King, R. H., and McKechnie: *Classical Mythology in Song and Story*. Toronto: Copp Clark, 1937

Knudtson, Peter, and David Suzuki. *Wisdom of the Elders*. Toronto: Stoddart, 1992.

Larson, Douglas, Uta Matthes, Peter E. Kelly, Jeremy Lundholm, and John Gerrath. *The Urban Cliff Revolution: New Findings on the Origins and Evolution of Human Habitats*. Markham: Fitzhenry and Whiteside, 2004.

Lima, Patrick. *The Art of Perennial Gardening: Creative Ways with Hardy Flowers*. Willowdale: Firefly Books, 1998.

Marks, Cassandra. *Homeopathy: A Step-by-Step Guide*. Shaftesbury, Dorset: Element Books, 1997.

Maynard, Mack, Leonard Dean, William Frost, ed. *Modern Poetry*. Englewood Cliffs: Prentice-Hall, 1950.

Menchu, Rigoberta. *I, Rigoberta Menchu: An Indian Woman in Guatemala*. Edited by Elisabeth Burgos-Debray. Translated by Ann Wright. London: Verso, 1984.

O'Driscoll, Herbert: *The Leap of the Deer: Memories of a Celtic Childhood*. Boston: Cowley Publications, 1994.

Ruether, Rosemary Radford. *Gaia and God: An Ecofeminist Theology of Earth Healing*. New York: HarperSanFrancisco, 1992.

Strong, Roy. *Small Period Gardens: A Practical Guide to Design and Planting*. Toronto: Stoddart, 1992.

The Holy Bible, New Revised Standard Version. Nashville: Thomas Nelson Publishers, 1989.

Visser, Margaret. *Much Depends on Dinner*. Toronto: HarperPerennial, 1992.

von Baeyer, Edwinna. *Rhetoric and Roses: A History of Canadian Gardening*. Markham: Fitzhenry and Whiteside, 1984.

Walker, Barbara. *The Woman's Encyclopedia of Myths and Secrets*. New York: HarperSanFrancisco, 1983.

Wright, Ronald. *A Short History of Progress*. Toronto: Anansi, 2004.

www.gardendigest.com *The Spirit of Gardening* website, created by Michael Garofalo.

Websites:

Government of Canada Climate Change. www.climatechange.gc.ca

Go for Green Canada. www.goforgreen.ca/gardening

City Farmer. www.cityfarmer.org

David Suzuki. www.davidsuzuki.org

Permissions & Photo Credits

Permission has been obtained to reproduce excerpts from the following works.

The Whole Earth Shall Cry Glory: Iona Prayers by Rev. George F. MacLeod © 1985 Wild Goose Publications, The Iona Community, 4th Floor Savoy House, 140 Sauchiehall Street, Glasgow G2 3DH. www.ionabooks.com

"The Autumn Sonnets" copyright © 1972 by May Sarton, from *Collected Poems 1930–1993* by May Sarton. Used by permission of W. W. Norton & Company, Inc.

"In Windsor, Ontario on Baba's 85th Birthday" © 1992 by Laurie Kruk, from *Theories of the World*. Used by permission of the author.

"There Is No Middle Ground" copyright © 1992 by Arthur Solomon, from *Songs for the People: Teachings on the Natural Way*. Used by permission of Eva Solomon.

"There Is No Place" copyright © D. G. Jones from *A Throw of Particles*. Used by permission of the author.

"The Seven of Pentacles" from *Circles on the Water* by Marge Piercy, copyright © 1982 by Marge Piercy. Used by permission of Alfred A. Knopf, a division of Random House, Inc.

Excerpt from "A Poem about a Story, and Other Things I Found in My Guestroom at Sooke, BC" from *Writing the Sacred: A Psalm-Inspired Path to Appreciating and Writing Sacred Poetry*, copyright © Ray McGinnis. Published by Northstone Publishing, 2005. Used by permission of the publisher.

History of Gardening Timeline © Michael Garofalo. www.gardendigest.com. Used by permission.

Dust Jacket
front cover: www.photos.com
back cover: Joyce DeMeester
left flap: www.photos.com (top), Margaret Kyle (bottom)
author photo: Wayne Singleton

Julie Bachewich: 42

Allan "Bow" Beauchamp: 31, as seen on the Tracker Trail website, www.trackertrail.com

Joyce DeMeester: 48, (gardener – 82, 119, 120, 121)

Julie Elliot: 127, 131

Karen Kranabetter: 77, (linocuts 159)

Margaret Kyle: (stepping stones – 8, 21, 41, 97, 137, 144), 11, (honeysuckle – 9, 153), 39, 40, 76, 89, 99, 108, 109, 118, 123, 136, 143, 153, (patio of Lois Huey-Heck and Jim Kalnin – 33, 70, 71, 84, 85)

Pati Mathias: 37, 103, owner of Clay Bank Farm Lavender, Naramata, BC, www.claybankfarmlavender.com,

Bob McCoubrey, McCoubrey's Organic Farm, Lake Country, BC: (pear – 9), 30, (sunflower – 51). See www.urbanharvest.ca/farmprofiles/farmprofiles.html

Roz Monita: 72, (tree peony – 79, 111), (Okanagan Lavender Herb Farm – 142)

Bonnie Schlosser: 62, 64

Michael Schwartzentruber: 7, 23, 41, (tulip and thistle – 51), 52, 80, 94, 146, (Halifax veranda –147), 152

Eva Schwartzentruber: 151

Donna Sinclair: 6, 8, (lily –10)

James Taylor: 13, 158

Ingrid Turnbull: 141

Mel Turnbull: 73

Spiro Vouladakis: 92, 96, (poppies – 93), 104, 138, 140

John Wallace: 10, 38, 100, 101, 134, 135

www.designpics.com: 29

www.photos.com: 1, 2 & 3, 4 & 5, 12, 14–22, 24, 25, 26–28, 32–36, 43, 44–47, 49–51, 53–59, 60–61, 63, 65–69, 74, 75, 78, 79, 81–83, 86–88, 90, 91, (butterfly – 93), 95, 97–98, 102, 105–107, 110, 112–117, 122, 124–126, 128–130, 132, 133, (creeping phlox – 144), 147–150, 154–157, 160

159